On the Road in an RV

Richard Dunlop

An AARP Book
published by
American Association of Retired Persons
Washington, D.C.
Scott, Foresman and Company
Lifelong Learning Division
Glenview, Illinois

Photo and Illustration Credits

Cover photo, James Tallon/OUTDOOR EXPOSURES

3, 19, 23, 33, 37, 43, 47, 48, 49, 50, 57, 65, 75, 89, 97, 115, 131, 143, 147, 151, 167, reprinted with the permission of the Recreation Vehicle Industry Association; 6, 8, from the collection of Henry Ford Museum and Greenwich Village; 11, courtesy Airstream; 30, 66, 116, Joan Dunlop; 39, 41, Coleman Company Photo; 44, 45, 134, courtesy Fleetwood, Inc.; 51, courtesy Komfort Motor Homes; 82, from the 1986 *Rand McNally Road Atlas,* © Rand McNally & Company, RL-87-S-19; 91, courtesy National Safety Council; 148, courtesy Family Motor Coach Association

Library of Congress Cataloging-in-Publication Data

Dunlop, Richard.
    On the road in an RV.

    Includes index.
    1. Recreational vehicles. 2. Mobile home living. I. Title.
TL298.D86   1987   796.7'9   86-31423
ISBN 0-673-24839-9

Contents

viii   Contents

Acknowledgments

No book that portrays the tremendous impact of recreation vehicles on how Americans spend their leisure and vacation time could be written without the help of a great number of informed people. The author appreciates the friendly assistance of hundreds of RV campers throughout the United States who have offered him everything from a cup of coffee or a jumper cable to their expert views on just what kind of campground is suited for just what purpose or what to do if a passing truck causes a trailer to sway.

Organizations have been extraordinarily helpful. The author wishes to thank these organizations, both public and private: Bureau of Land Management, European Travel Commission, Family Motor Coach Association, Good Sam RV Owners Club, Loners on Wheels, Mexican Government Tourist Office, National Campers and Hikers Association, National Campground Owners Association, National Forest Service, National Institute for Automotive Service Excellence, National Parks Service, National Safety Council, Parks Canada, Recreation Vehicle Industry Association, Recreation Vehicle Rental Association, Tourism Canada, U.S. Army Corps of Engineers, U.S. Fish and Wildlife Service, and Virginia Division of Motor Vehicles.

The American Association of Retired Persons has been very supportive from the start. The author would particularly like to express his appreciation to such AARP people as Bob Forbes, Hal Norvell, Barbara Alderman, and Marion and Donald Waite, who first saw the importance of a book that would bring together for the first time the many aspects of RV living.

Introduction

The nomadic instinct in Americans did not suddenly bloom in the prosperous years after World War II. It came ashore with the first settlers at Jamestown and Plymouth and was nurtured on the colonial streets of Penn's Green City of Philadelphia and Dutch New Amsterdam. Daniel Boone was a boy on a farm in Bucks County, not far from Philadelphia, and he exemplified the westering American, who always had to see what lay just over the next mountain range, within the mysterious forests, across the beckoning plains, beyond the Great Lakes, and along the most remote river torrents.

It is no coincidence that the Conestoga wagon, the covered wagon of America's pioneer trails and wagon roads, was also born near Philadelphia in Lancaster County. In a real way the covered wagon of the pioneers was the forerunner of today's recreational vehicles, though the RVs encountered on the contemporary interstates and in campgrounds seem more likely to have been designed by Jules Verne than by descendants of the wagon builders.

"An emigrant should travel light," advised Joel Palmer, who journeyed over the Oregon Trail in 1845, but this admonition didn't keep him from suggesting that a pioneer bring along a sheet-iron stove; a Dutch oven; a cast-metal skillet; tin plates, cups, and saucers; two churns, one for sweet and one for sour milk; a keg for water; implements such as a handsaw, plow mold, ax, shovel, rope; and a rifle and shotgun. RV travelers may have different priorities as to what they think is important to include in their rig, but at least they share the covered wagon traveler's desire to travel light.

A few years ago my teenaged son Rick and I followed the Oregon Trail in a truck camper all the way from St. Joseph, Missouri, to trail's end at The Dalles in Oregon.

"Our truck camper's a lot like a covered wagon," observed Rick as we set up camp at Ash Hollow, Nebraska, where the very ruts of the covered wagons could still be seen etched into a nearby hillside. "We've got all we need on wheels."

This might well have been questioned, but we were indeed using a truck camper on the trip because it was self-contained. We were boondocking, as RV travelers would say, stopping wherever we wished on our journey through time and space. Essentially Rick was right, and I've heard other RV travelers, some in simple pop-up trailers, others in elaborate forty-foot motor homes, compare their vehicles to the wagons of the pioneers.

A few years later while camping along the historic Mullan Military Road in Montana with my family, we came upon four pioneer wagons, forlorn and deserted beside a gravel ranch road just south of Fort Shaw. Our modern family confronted the vehicles of yesterday's pioneers. We took pictures and hoped that a museum's agents would come out into this lonely country and find the wagons before vandals did. Then with a blast of our horn in salute we drove on.

1
America on Wheels

How many of today's Americans share the pioneer's nomadic life? According to Gary LaBella, a vice president of the Recreation Vehicle Industry Association (RVIA), twenty-five million Americans (nearly one-third, fifty years or older) enjoy the RV lifestyle. They do so because an RV allows travelers to go where they want when they want and provides a place to live on the way and when they arrive. What's more, they can prepare their own meals. It is no wonder that with an RV Americans cannot withstand the lure of the open road. As John Steinbeck expressed in his *Travels with Charley,* Americans have a hunger "to go someday, to move about, free and unanchored, not toward something but away from something."

The Go Camping America Committee puts it more completely if more prosaically: "Camping's appeal is very basic, which is why people of all ages and all social and economic backgrounds are attracted to it. For those seeking adventure and excitement, it's forever at their fingertips. For those who want solitude, there's no better place to find it than in the outdoors. For those wishing to reduce stress and promote their health, camping offers opportunities for enjoying physical activities such as hiking and swimming. For everyone searching for an economical leisure-time pursuit and one that can help draw their family closer together, camping is it."

The A. C. Neilsen Company, which polls Americans about virtually every subject that comes to mind, discovered in 1982 that camping is third only to swimming and fishing in popularity among American adults. For children under twelve years of age, camping finished third, after swimming and bicycling.

Camping is more popular than bowling, boating, jogging, softball, tennis, skiing, hunting, golf, ice skating, soccer, and billiards, which helps explain why, generation after generation Scouting remains the most popular of all youth activities. According to Neilsen more than 61 million Americans, one out of every four persons, went camping in 1982. By 1990 the number is expected to swell to 64.4 million. Moms, dads, kids, grandmas, and grandpas all go camping, and campers include such people as doctors, plumbers, corporation executives, grocers, and construction workers—all of whom cherish the fact that at a campsite there are no phones and no worries and relaxation comes easy.

The Neilsen study also showed that among campers, those who prefer tents are most numerous, at 44.6 percent; RV campers come next, at 39.1 percent; and backpackers are last, with 11.1 percent. Since some RV campers also backpack or pitch a tent on occasion and some backpackers see no problem in driving to trail head in an RV, there is a great deal of crossover in camping categories that Neilsen's studies do not indicate. In 1985 another study made by the University of Michigan Survey Research Center showed that one in every ten vehicle-owning American families now owns an RV, with the greatest growth in ownership taking place among people between thirty-five and fifty-four years of age, the prime family years.

It is not surprising that there are more than sixteen thousand campgrounds in this country. Some eight thousand are public campgrounds in national and state parks, forests, and other public lands, and eight thousand are privately owned. Campgrounds range from a place to park a rig for the night, cheek by jowl with other rigs, on a pull-through space close to the rushing traffic of an interstate to a remote spot provided by the Bureau of Land Management high on a mountain shoulder overlooking the vast flats of Alamogordo in New Mexico. Some are spartan, with no connections for an RV's utilities, and others compare in their facilities with the plushest resorts.

Pioneer RVers

The value of RVs sold in the United States every year runs around eight billion dollars. Scarcely anyone would have expected such enormous growth in the 1930s, when, in the depths of the Depression, John Steinbeck made his first youthful trip in what he later called "an old bakery wagon, double-doored rattler with mattress on its floor." Steinbeck, with all his zest for RV travel, scarcely was the first American to camp in a truck. Most likely the honors go to Henry B. Joy, president of the Packard Motor Car Company. At 5:00 P.M. on Monday, March 20, 1916, Packard received a telephone order from the War Department in Washington for twenty-seven Packard "war trucks." Workmen labored throughout the night to build the vehicles, and within twenty-two hours they were aboard a fourteen-car train headed for the Mexican border where Pancho Villa had raided the United States. General John J. Pershing intended to use the vehicles in his pursuit of Pancho Villa into Mexico. Equipping one of the trucks with cots, stove, and cooking utensils, Harry Joy and William R. McCulla, a Packard engineer, drove to Mexico themselves to see how the hot pursuit was going. Later Joy used the truck camper for camping trips with his family. Today this twelve-cylinder vehicle, a gift of Henry Joy, is displayed in the Henry Ford Museum in Dearborn, Michigan.

Not far away in the museum is still another pioneer RV. Beginning in 1915, Henry Ford went on annual motor caravan odysseys to such places as the Blue Ridge Mountains, the Adirondacks, New England, and northern Michigan. A White truck carried the equipment and supplies, and several automobiles accommodated the "vagabonds," as Ford called such guests as Harvey Firestone, John Burroughs, and

A 1921 White Truck

Thomas A. Edison. In 1921 the vagabonds were joined by President Warren G. Harding complete with a Secret Service contingent, so the expedition must have been a remarkable thing to behold as it set up camp by a wilderness stream. The Henry Ford Museum also displays a 1922 Lincoln camping truck, which had not only a refrigerator but also compartments for tools and utensils. Henry Ford, who considered himself no mean cook, often prepared pancakes in this early-day RV.

In 1986 the National Museum of American History at the Smithsonian Institution in Washington opened an exhibit entitled, At Home on the Road: Autocamping, Motels, and the Rediscovery of America. Among the vehicles displayed was a 1928 green canvas folding Gilkie tent trailer with antique Coleman equipment. To celebrate the occasion, a veteran RVer, David Woodworth, who loaned the Coleman gear to the Smithsonian, went on a cross-country trip through the United States in his 1928 Ford touring car, pulling a rare Zagelmeyer trailer dating from the 1920s.

Ray Harroun, winner of the first Indianapolis 500-mile race in 1911, made a two-wheel house trailer in 1936 and traveled in it, and Charles A. Lindbergh often went camping in a Gilkie tent trailer, which he gave up in 1942 in favor of a Stage Coach trailer. This twenty-three-foot-long trailer was built by the Ideal Manufacturing Corporation of Mishawaka, Indiana, in 1935 and purchased by Henry Ford for the Henry Ford Museum as a demonstration of contemporary travel trends. The trailer boasted electric lights, a stove, an ice box, a sink, a lavatory, convertible beds, and storage closets and was considered way ahead of its time. When Lindbergh mentioned to Ford that he was thinking of buying a trailer to pull behind his 1940 Mercury station wagon so that he could "get away

A 1935 Stage Coach Trailer

from it all" to do some studying and writing, Ford withdrew the trailer from the museum and gave it to the aviator, who traveled through thirty-nine states and Ontario, Canada, over the next fifteen years. In 1957 Lindbergh repainted the canvas roof and returned the trailer to the museum, where it still can be seen.

The First Camping Trailers

The first camping trailers were put together by do-it-yourselfers in their backyards. As a typical example, Angelo Novo of Santa Maria, a small California town, created a teardrop trailer with sweeping curves that featured portholes instead of windows. He finished the trailer's interior with varnished plywood and covered the plywood floor with linoleum. A sink with water under air pressure, a small gasoline stove, an ice box, a closet, and a double bed gave Novo a comfortable alternative to tent camping.

One of the first to build trailers on a commercial scale was J. Paul Getty, who fashioned them out of scrap metal from his aircraft factory, but Wally Byam, an advertising agency executive in Los Angeles and would-be magazine publisher, was the first to realize the potential in RV travel. When Byam was a boy in Baker, Oregon, his grandfather took him along on freight trains pulled by sixteen-mule teams to the Colorado river. Later, as a teenaged shepherd in the Oregon mountains, Byam lived in a two-wheel wagon covered with cloth and towed by a donkey. At night he unhitched the donkey and propped the wagon firmly in place by its tongue. He let down the tailboard so that he could get at a kerosene cookstove, his food supplies and water, and a mat where he slept.

As Byam told friends later in life, his youthful experiences led him to construct in his backyard what he later described as a "crude, boxy structure which rested none too easily upon a Model A Ford chassis." The trailer offered "little more than a bed you could crawl into, a shelf to hold a water bottle, a flashlight and some camping equipment, protected from the elements." When neighbors tried to buy the trailer from him, he wrote an article on how to build a trailer for less than one hundred dollars and published it in *Popular Mechanics* magazine. He also sold plans to his trailer and in 1930 began to produce made-to-order examples for sale. In 1934 he called the teardrop-shaped trailers he was building Airstream, "because that's the way they travel, like a stream of air." Each trailer that Byam finished was said to be an improvement over the one before. He gave up building his trailers of plywood and Masonite and constructed them of aluminum alloy. He added water pumps, chemical toilets, ice boxes, and gasoline stoves and designed the trailers' shapes to improve towability and mileage.

When he introduced the Clipper in January 1936, Byam gave the nation's nomads their first best-selling RV. Resembling an airplane and built of riveted aluminum, it slept four and featured a tubular frame dinette, seats that converted into beds, a water supply, cabinets, and a galley. It was, as Byam's sales brochures pointed out, "completely equipped with electric lights" and employed dry ice in an air-conditioning system. The original Clipper, nicknamed "Grand Dad," is kept on display at the Airstream factory at Jackson Center, Ohio. It cost twelve thousand dollars in the depth of the Depression, but Byam could not keep up with the demand. America was ready to take to the open road.

The Wally Byam Clubs

Some Airstreamers would also like to maintain that Wally Byam started the first RV club, but the honor probably goes to a Chicagoan, Jim Morrison, who in the 1920s formed Tin Can Tourists of the World for travelers who had built their own trailers, usually with a metallic surface or at least a surface painted to resemble metal. Most likely the Tin Can Tourists took their name from the appearance of their trailers, but there are some who maintain that they got the name because they tied tin cans to their trailers' axles. If the trailer had a flat tire, the tin can clanked to let the driver know.

The Tin Can Tourists and their like grew in numbers every year until 1941, when the Japanese attack on Pearl Harbor brought an end to the burgeoning RV industry's use of aluminum alloy. Fuel and tires were rationed, and Byam himself went to work for a Los Angeles aircraft plant. He found his wartime employment valuable when, with the defeat of the Axis, he returned to making his Airstream trailers in a building near the Van Nuys, California, airport. Other manufacturers soon were springing up to share in post–World War II America's economic growth.

Byam has made one more important contribution to RV travel. In 1951 he went barnstorming through Central America, all the way to Panama, as wagon master of a caravan of Airstream trailers, and the Wally Byam caravan was born. The next year he led a larger caravan through Mexico and up the West Coast of the United States. On a 1955 caravan to eastern Canada, the Airstreamers formed the Wally Byam Club, which exists to this day.

Byam also led five hundred trailers into Mexico in 1955; the first trailer was already two hundred miles south of the Mexican border when, at a rate of three a minute, the last of them were still passing through customs. Later Byam caravans toured Europe and the Soviet Union, and trekked from Cape Town to Cairo through Africa. At night on the African journey, Air-

An RV caravan shares a spot with a camel caravan near Luxor, Egypt.

streamers circled their trailers and built bonfires in the middle to keep off prowling animals. They thought nothing of fixing flat tires four or five times a day, had an audience with Emperor Haile Selassie of Ethiopia, and at last arrived in Cairo, where in triumph they surrounded the Great Pyramids. In the last few years Airstreamers have journeyed through China in trailers that, with the completion of the final trip, will be presented to the Chinese people. Wally Byam died in 1962, but his spirit still goes traveling with his caravans, as confident as ever that RV travel in foreign lands creates bonds of international understanding.

The First Motor Homes

It was not until the 1960s that the first motor homes were built. At first they were too expensive for most people, but as production expanded, manufacturers brought the prices down, and today they have taken over a good part of the RV market. A University of Michigan survey conducted in 1985 established that of the 7 million American households with RVs, 14 percent owned motor homes and 17 percent van campers, 35 percent fifth-wheel trailers or travel trailers, 14 percent folding camping trailers, and 20 percent truck campers.

The Lure of RVs

RV camping has become popular for many reasons. David J. Humphreys, president of the Recreation Vehicle Industry Association, states a number of key factors: a favorable economic climate, low gas prices and interest rates, increasing consumer preference for domestic travel, and demographic information that shows a bigger portion of the population moving into the peak ownership age groups.

A study of the RV industry in the 1980s by public opinion researchers Yankelovich, Skelly, and White points up the importance of the leisure ethic in shaping how Americans choose to spend their lives.

"The baby boom generation was acculturated to the leisure ethic," concludes the survey. "And the older segments of the population show signs of heightened interest in leisure as many enjoy early retirement with good financial and physical health."

But why RV travel instead of more traditional ways to vacation? Unlike people who are traveling on airlines, buses, or trains, RVers can set their own pace. If they wake up to a rainy day, they may just roll over in their comfortable RV bed and say to themselves "We don't like driving in the rain, so we'll just stay a day longer in camp." RV travelers operate on "Indian time." When our family was camping on the Oglala Sioux Reservation at Pine Ridge, South Dakota, a chief made arrangements for a guide to show us a fossil area on Red Shirt Table.

"When we say we are going to come and guide you to a place where you can look for fossils at ten o'clock, that means we'll be there anywhere from eleven to twelve o'clock," he said. "That's what we mean by Indian time."

A Texan RV traveler whom we met in a campground in Land Between the Lakes, Kentucky, put the matter of time more pungently. He quoted Vice President John Nance Garner: "Don't hurry, don't hurry. It's better to be late at the Golden Gate than to get to Hell on time."

RV travelers will tell you that they not only go where they want, when they want, but they are free from worry about lost luggage, crowded air and rail terminals, lost reservations, hotel checkout times, and unappetizing restaurant meals. Betty and Fred Marker, a retired couple who live in Englewood, Florida, explained, "After taking suitcases in and out of something like forty hotels and motels in sixty-five days, we decided there had to be a better way."

The better way to the Markers and several millions of their fellow American travelers is the RV way, in which clothes hang in closets or are kept in drawers exactly as if they were at home. While other people are standing in line at a check-in counter in an airport or waiting for a waiter to bring them a meal, an RV traveler may well be camped by the side of a mountain lake, sipping a glass of wine while dinner is cooking on the stove or in the microwave. RV travelers are the kind who prize the out-of-doors, the serenity of a wilderness setting, and the sense that in the next campground there are bound to be friendly and agreeable people who will be helpful if help is needed.

Of course, some RV travelers prefer plush accommodations such as might be expected in a top resort, and as a result camp resorts are now common throughout the nation. RVers can choose from campgrounds as primitive as those in a national forest or Bureau of Land Management area or camp resorts, where such amenities as a fish-stocked lake, a swimming pool, a golf course, tennis and racquetball courts, a clubhouse, and a health club come with the hookups.

Saving Money

RV travel is also easier on the pocketbook than any other travel. In 1985 Pannell Kerr Forster, an international firm of certified public accountants specializing in the hospitality industries, compared vacation costs and determined that travel by RV on the average costs 50 percent less than car and hotel and motel vacations, 67 percent less than bus and train and hotel and motel trips, and 75 percent less than air and hotel and motel trips. They discovered that a family of four taking an average eight-night vacation would spend $512 using the most costly RV, staying at campgrounds, and cooking most of their meals in their vehicle or over a campfire. The same family traveling in their own car, staying in one motel or hotel room, and eating most of their meals in restaurants would spend $1,055. The equivalent bus trip cost $1,527; train trip, $1,534; and air trip, $1,946. With the sharp decline in gasoline prices since the study was made, RV vacations compare even more favorably with other kinds of travel in terms of cost.

The newest RVs get considerably better mileage than the old gas guzzlers of preenergy-crunch days, but the out-of-pocket expense of driving a vehicle from one spot to another still makes up a good part of the cost of an RV trip. The biggest savings are made in accommodations and meals. Meals cost no more than at home when a family cooks in its own RV, and in 1985 an average campground fee was a bit less than eleven dollars per night compared with about fifty-four dollars per night for an average hotel room. Of course, there are a lot of hotel rooms that cost less than the average, but then for campers who don't need the hookups and amenities of a commercial campsite, costs run anywhere from nothing at all to a few dollars.

In 1984 the United States Auto Club sent John and Sandy Banks and their two teenaged sons on a vacation trip from California to the Grand Canyon. On the outward-bound trip, they traveled in their new sedan, stopped overnight at motels, and ate their meals in restaurants. When they reached the Grand Canyon, they hooked a folding camping trailer behind their car and returned over exactly the same route, stopping at the same towns. This time they camped in private and public campgrounds, prepared their own meals, and ate either in their trailer or on picnic tables. Their second week cost them $462.00 less than their first week. In Las Vegas on the first leg of the trip the Banks family rented a fifth-floor motel room for $33.92 per night, and one week later they paid $7.42 for a campsite just next door. At the Grand Canyon, they spent $60.00 a night for a room in the lodge and then moved into their trailer to spend their second night at the canyon at a campsite that cost $9.27. Since then motel and hotel rooms have gone up in price. Campgrounds cost more too, but RV travelers today soon discover that they can save a great deal of money if they camp instead of spend their nights in the inn.

The Yankelovich, Skelly, and White study also shows that today's American lifestyle is conducive to the purchase of a recreation vehicle, since over time it is perceived to "give value, options, and a variety of leisure experiences." Few would contest this, but there are also many Americans who remember the energy crunch of 1973. What might happen if there is another major upset in the volatile Middle East and oil again is in short supply? Today the United States is far less dependent on foreign oil supplies and has cut its consumption of petroleum products 11 percent since 1980. RV owners found a 1986 report, "World Petroleum Resources—A Perspective," issued by the Department of the Interior to be reassuring.

"World oil and gas resources appear to be in such quantity," stated the report, "as to ensure significant availability until about the middle of the 21st century." The report admitted that potential war or political boycotts growing out of Middle East tensions might yet cause U.S. RV travelers trouble, but every year the United States moves closer to energy independence. In seventy-five years, the report concludes, oil production will not matter because the production of fuel from coal or power from uranium will propel our vehicles and heat homes. Meanwhile prospective RV buyers have made it very clear that fuel economy is one of the qualities they demand of any recreation vehicle.

2
RVers' Lifestyle

Who are these RV recreationists? Sometimes they seem to be a tribe unto themselves. A study of Airstream owners indicates that they range in background from blue-collar workers to lawyers, ministers, and doctors; they have an average age of sixty; 85 percent no longer work every day; and they travel between ten and fifteen thousand miles a year. They are mostly white, but the numbers of blacks and Hispanics among them are increasing yearly. They have a passion for knowing where their fellow RV travelers are from, and they like to send out Christmas cards featuring a recreation vehicle in some way. Their credit is good. Fifty-one percent pay cash for their RVs, but when RV purchasers take out loans, the American Bankers Association reports, they have the best repayment rating among all consumer borrowers.

The late Supreme Court Justice William O. Douglas spoke for RVers when he said, "Man is whole when he is in tune with the winds, the stars, and the hills as well as with his neighbor. Being in tune with the apartment or the community is part of the secret. Being in tune with the universe is the entire secret."

RVers may not be able to live in the entire universe, but their lifestyle suggests that they can live in the entire world, or at least in all of North America. An RV camper is young in heart—an activist in life who believes in involvement with the environment but values independence and self-reliance.

"When you get out of the city and into the wilds, you hear the planet speak," said David Brower, the Sierra Club's first executive director, and RV campers would agree. They feel drawn closer to nature than their stay-at-home, city-confined fellow citizens, and they feel that they are healthier physically and mentally because of this closeness. There is little question also that most RV travelers make friends more readily than do other travelers—being friendly is part of their mindset. Our family has camped in hundreds of campgrounds, and we've rarely found unfriendly or thoughtless fellow campers.

One evening we pulled our rig into a campsite at Seminole Canyon State Park in west Texas. We needed a jumper cable to start our second vehicle, and almost immediately a man from British Columbia sauntered over with a cable in hand. When the motor roared alive, the Canadian and his wife sat down with us and tasted a bit of Texas wine we'd bought that afternoon from a winery at Del Rio, which is as old if not older than any in California's Napa Valley. That evening we were invited to their trailer for dessert. My wife, Joan, brought along her recorder. Our host got out his violin and played old Scottish reels and songs. When Joan joined in with her recorder, a thirteen-year-old boy from a nearby campsite came over carrying his own recorder and shyly began to play. We all sang and listened to the music of the violin and recorders. That night Joan and I walked back to our motor home past the campfires of other campers. The Texas stars above were indeed big and bright, and there was a serenity that is rarely found anywhere except in the outdoors.

Campground comradery is one of the most appealing aspects of RV travel, but RVers also are likely to make friends along the way. The Tigua Indian Reservation is fourteen miles down the Rio Grande from El Paso, Texas. Joan and I pulled our twenty-six-foot motor home towing a four-wheel-drive Bronco Two into a parking spot near the Tigua Visitor's Center. We traipsed indoors to watch teenaged Indian boys and girls dance a welcome to the tourists. At the end a grinning boy pranced to a stop in front of us, lifted his arms in imitation of a driver at the wheel of a motor home, and made engine noises. A small boy leaped behind him and seized his belt. Both boys, laughing over their shoulders, danced off after the others in unmistakable imitation of our motor home and its accompanying second vehicle.

Two families of migrant field workers proved just as friendly as the mischievous Indian boys when my thirteen-year-old son Rick and I parked our truck camper beneath some sheltering trees beside the pioneer Barlow Road on the shoulders of Oregon's Mount Hood. Once the Barlow Road was a key wagon road reaching from the end of the Oregon Trail at The Dalles over the southern flank of Mount Hood to the fertile Willamette Valley. The U.S. Forest Service keeps the road open as a fire road, and there is a string of wilderness campsites along it.

"We'll get half a dozen campers every month," a ranger had informed us. "I don't think you'll have to worry about being overcrowded."

The ranger also assured us that we would have no trouble getting through. Next to our truck camper the migrant workers set up their camp. Tired from picking pears in the orchards of the Hood River Valley, the men and women climbed dejectedly out of their weary cars, but their kids tumbled, barefoot and jubilant, out of the backseats and shouted and ran in search of firewood. There was a flurry of preparation for the night, with men and women shouting at the kids, cuffing one here and ordering another about there. Some boys ran to a boiling stream with cane poles and worms dangling on their hooks and came back with trout.

Rick and I followed the rocky stream with a few of the migrant boys.

"Got to look lively," said Billy, a twelve-year-old from the Missouri Ozarks. "Last year the water rushed a man over the falls."

When he saw signs of grizzly bear, which for some reason often come to the falls near the campground, we hurried back to camp.

"Got to build a fire to keep away the bears," said Billy's sinewy father.

We all gathered and chopped wood. As soon as the cooking was over, Rick and I shared our dessert with Billy's family. We sat around the roaring fire that, if not really needed to keep off the bears, at least gave us protection from the mountain chill that crept down from the high snowfields as soon as the sun set. Rick got out his guitar and played and sang mainly for the ears of two beautiful Ozark girls. I had seen the girls earlier in the evening watching the strange boy with the ready grin who traveled in a truck camper and who chopped wood and kindled their fire. They had gone to the stream and washed away the day's dust from their faces and bare legs. Now they listened to him sing and asked shyly for the same songs over and over. Then their father took Rick's guitar and picked out the old songs of the frontier.

"I planned on being a guitar picker back home in Missouri," he said, "and I ended up a pear picker."

We listened to the old songs, and the flames died down. The bright-eyed children and the mother nodding in her weariness seemed a picture materialized out of the Barlow Road's past. Billy came and sat next to me. He clutched a stick in his bare toes and held it to the fire until it burst into flame.

"My dog cured my asthma," he confided.

"Your dog, Billy?"

"Yes, my dog."

He turned a pleased face to me and undid a button on his shirt. A chihuahua's head poked out and lovingly licked the boy's chin. I had noticed the bulge in the boy's sacklike shirt, but I had not guessed that a dog lay hidden there.

RVers of all ages meet and socialize as they travel.

"I keep him warm at night because he hasn't got much hair," explained Billy. "I used to be right bad, but the doctor said I needed something to love. My daddy got me this dog, and my asthma went away."

I wondered how many pears had to be picked to pay for the little dog. The fire died down, and the night grew chilly. Billy's chihuahua crept back in his shirt, and we all went to the comfort of our blankets.

One of the reasons RV travelers make new friends as they travel is that they don't seem to be in a big hurry, and people along the way don't think they are imposing on them if they strike up a conversation. Veteran RVers know that it isn't how far they drive during the day that matters but how many worthwhile experiences they have on the day's journey. Small-town and country people who shy away from travelers possessed by the hurry bug are attracted to RVers.

RVers in Action

If most RVers say that people are what matters most to them in their travels, activities run a close second in appeal. Some RVers pan for gold or search for gemstones; others express their talent for arts and crafts, go in for hot-air ballooning or square dancing, or go fishing or birding. They golf, windsurf, attend seminars, participate in swap meetings, assist in wild horse roundups, snorkel, explore caves, and make their own soap if this so pleases them. Many of these activities, as well as others, are featured in such RV periodicals as *Family Motor Coaching* (PO Box 44144, Cincinnati, OH 45244) and *Motorhome* and *Trailer Life* (TL Enterprises, Inc., 29901 Agoura Road, Agoura, CA 91301).

There is even a Gem and Mineral Club for RVers,

which conducts field trips to such places as the Diamond Ledge collecting area near Herkimer, New York. Gem-collecting RVers in the Midwest know that the Crater of Diamonds State Park near Murfreesboro, Akansas, is a good place to set up their rigs, since it is close to the only diamond mine in North America. They soon discover that a diamond can be a rockhound's best friend. A Dallas, Texas, woman paid the nominal prospector's fee and scrounged about in the clay. She discovered what appeared to be a large piece of a broken Coca-Cola bottle and might have flung it away, but a ranger geologist on duty told her it was a diamond.

The lady took the diamond to an appraiser at home, who assured her it was very valuable. She couldn't believe her good luck and showed it to an appraiser in New York City. He judged the stone to weigh fifteen carats and be worth around $75,000.

When looking for diamonds, it is a good idea to take along some children. Whether it's because their eyesight is sharper, their eyes are closer to the ground, or their concentration is better, kids find far more diamonds than do grown-ups.

An electrician from Pine Bluff, Arkansas, took his family to the Crater of Diamonds. He had no luck whatsoever, and he was about to head for home when his toddler daughter picked up a stone and put it in her mouth. Afraid that she might choke, he fished the stone out of her jaws with a probing finger. When he showed it to the ranger on duty, he was told he had a diamond. It turned out to be worth five thousand dollars.

No Generation Gap

Children can be very comfortable on an RV vacation. Tom Bowens, director of Bays Mountain Park, at

Kingsport, Tennessee, likes to promote this mixing of generations. He allows people over sixty-five and under sixteen to fish in his reservoir.

"The two age groups work well together," he explains, and most grandparents and many parents will agree. Some older RVers don't care to travel with their grandchildren, but others insist that it is the way to go. They not only have sharper eyes that come in handy for spotting diamonds (to say nothing of fast food restaurants and campgrounds with swimming pools), but they also bring a fresh sense of discovery to a trip. RV travel fascinates most kids, partly because they are far less confined than they would be in an automobile. On the road they can play games ranging from License Plate Poker to Bury the Cow, which purportedly was invented by a hard-pressed grandmother in California. To play the latter game, players count the cows they see on a given side of the road. When they pass a cemetery on their side, they must bury all the counted cows and start over again. A time limit of perhaps an hour is set to decide the winner—the person who counts the most cows.

Some RVers take their kids on trips to broaden their education. We met a teacher in Australia who was taking his twelve-year-old son on a six-month RV trip over the road that reaches entirely around that nation's coast.

"He'll learn far more than he ever would in school," explained the teacher, who was able to supplement these road lessons with the more formal school lessons.

Recently on the Navajo Indian Reservation of Arizona we pulled our motor home up next to one driven by a doctor and his wife from Louisiana. We walked out on the desert with a Navajo guide to search for dinosaur footprints and met the doctor and his wife with their three sons and a daughter, who were excitedly looking for the footprints and bringing their parents all sorts of desert minerals and blooms for instant lessons in geology and flora. The doctor told us that he had taken his kids out of school, since his wife and he had come to the conclusion that they could educate them better themselves. We agreed that he might well have a point when we saw their boys putting their hands on an actual dinosaur track. It certainly beat reading about it in a book. Later in Monument Valley we encountered the same family. They had been visiting an Indian hogan, and a loving Navajo grandmother had tied the little girl's hair in an Indian girl's style. The girl had just bought in the trading post an Indian doll that had its hair tied the same way, and she proudly pointed to her doll's hair and to her own. Travel with adults who have a flair for teaching can be a very valuable experience for kids, and RV travel with its freedom from schedules is particularly attractive to youngsters.

Camping Solo

Some RVers may prefer to travel with kids or at least with other people, but Virginia Marth of Elsinore, Missouri, camps alone. She drives her camper van to meetings of Loners on Wheels and edits the group's newsletters for 3,800 members in all fifty states as well as Canada, Australia, and England. The Loners may travel alone, but they enjoy getting together for campouts where they play cards, cook out, fish, and above all, talk.

Some RVers who travel alone prefer to camp in private campgrounds because they feel that they are more secure. They believe that many public campgrounds are not patrolled well enough for a single person to be safe. A few loners even camp most of the time in membership-only campgrounds because they feel they are the best patrolled of all. For the most part, single campers do not go off into remote areas and camp by themselves. They prefer to have good campground neighbors handy in case of trouble. Probably most important of all, a loner on wheels does not stay alone very long. The friendliness and comradery of RV people are very real, and a trip that may begin alone soon can become an adventure in making friends.

Combining Business with Pleasure

Most RV travelers in the 1980s are either families with school-age children or senior citizens, but there are also a large number of young singles and people who find RV travel practical for business purposes. Stuart Anderson, who owns the Black Angus Cattle Company restaurant chain, travels to his 102 restaurants in sixteen states in a motor home.

"The difference between staying in our motor coach and in a hotel," says Anderson, "is that a hotel is so impersonal. In the coach my wife, Helen, can prepare a home-cooked meal. And we've got all the little personal things with us. In other words, it's home."

Construction workers who have to move from place to place find RV living both practical and satisfying, and so do some politicians, who in their pursuit of votes travel thousands of miles. George Makas, a Northfield, Illinois, musician who represents the Institute of Holyland Studies, travels from twelve to sixteen weeks a year in his motor home. His wife, Jean, has an electric piano in their rig so that she can keep in practice for the recitals that George, who plays the violin, and she give on college campuses. Rock groups frequently travel in RVs and so did TV personality Charles Kuralt in his search for offbeat America. People who use RVs for business travel also may write off at least part of the cost against their gross income when it comes to the annual rendezvous with the Internal Revenue Service.

Sometimes senior citizens who travel in RVs combine business with pleasure, but in the main they are happy to be retired. Robert J. Forbes, director of the American Association of Retired Persons (AARP) Special Services Department, told a recent Annual Travel Outlook Forum that statistics and research drawn from several sources and collated by the AARP show that people aged fifty and older travel in much the same way that younger people do. To his listeners' surprise, he showed that there is almost no difference in the time of year that older and younger people take their trips, and seniors tend to go just about everywhere that younger people go. The big difference is that older people as a rule spend almost twice as long away from home as do younger travelers. Stereotypes about senior RV travel simply do not hold up when scrutinized. Today people are retiring earlier and at the same time keeping a part-time interest in their affairs so that retirement is not necessarily as full a break as it was in previous generations. All of this is reflected in contemporary patterns of RV travel.

Snowbirds and Full-timers

That older RV travelers may go to the same places but stay longer is particularly true of the snowbirds, or as they are called in Texas, "winter Texans," who annually migrate from their homes in the North to sunny campgrounds in the Rio Grande Valley. One RV campground owner made a count of the 375 RV parks in the valley and their 57,000 spaces. He estimated that 114,000 snowbirds were happily escaping the snows. Still other snowbirds winter in the desert Southwest or in Florida. In the California desert, people also refer to the rainbirds, who every year flee the rains of the Pacific Northwest and British Columbia. From October to April the annual migration of RV travelers has become one of the social phenomena of the 1980s, and its economic and social impact has yet to be fully assessed.

Some of the RV migrants are what are called full-timers. They may have a summer cottage in the North, but many have no other home than their RV. Tired of being tied to a home that they feel they no longer need, weary of tax assessments and the costs of maintenance and mortgages, and disturbed by the seeming or real

The Western Way Resort in Tucson, Arizona, where RVers sometimes settle in for months at a time.

coldness of the communities they once called home, full-timers go where they want to go. The University of Michigan report showed that half of all RV owners spend from one to four months in their units, but that only 5 percent are full-timers. Although they may not make up a statistically large proportion of RV travelers, their mystique and their sometimes feisty adherence to their chosen lifestyle give them presence far beyond what the numbers might suggest.

One thing is certain: RV travelers—whether snowbirds, full-timers, or people who simply prefer to travel in an RV on their family vacations—all share a common desire to escape from the hassles and high costs of more structured travel. They share a tent camper's wish to be at home in nature, and they carry on the American tradition of volunteerism. RV travelers can be found serving in national parks and forests as unpaid campground hosts, fire watchers, and wildlife counters. They save the national treasury millions of dollars every year and thoroughly enjoy what they are doing. In Baja California a group of doctors who travel by RV take care of indigent villagers at no charge, and members of the Good Sam Club in Houston, Texas, take youngsters suffering from cancer on fishing expeditions and to summer camp. It is said in the desert Southwest, along the Rio Grande of Texas, and in Florida that if all the snowbirds stayed home, these areas would lose a very large proportion of their volunteer librarians, day-care workers, and just plain "I'm ready to help out wherever I can" citizens. Every study shows that the instinct to be a good neighbor exists in RV travelers side by side with the nomadic instinct. This was true on the American frontier of yesterday, and it is true on the highways and in the campgrounds of today.

3
Choosing an RV

When author John Steinbeck prepared in 1961 for his now celebrated book *Travels with Charley,* he remarked, "I wrote to the head office of a great corporation which manufactures trucks. I specified my purpose and my needs. I wanted a three-quarter-ton pick-up truck, capable of going anywhere under possibly rigorous conditions, and on this truck I wanted a little house built like the cabin of a small boat."

In due course he took delivery on a truck camper with a built-in double bed, four-burner stove, heater, refrigerator, electric lights, chemical toilet, closet, space for storage, and screened windows.

Bewildering Variety of RVs

It is not quite that easy to pick an RV today because there are some 233 manufacturers making a bewildering variety of travel trailers, fifth-wheel travel trailers, folding camping trailers, truck campers, motor homes, van campers, mini motor homes, and van conversions ranging in price from a few thousand dollars to a half million. Taken all together, there is something for virtually every travel lifestyle, and the trick in buying an RV is to make sure that the vehicle purchased fits your own recreational plans, as well as your pocketbook.

At one extreme is the folding camping trailer, favored by cost-conscious young families who want to live close to the sounds and scents of nature. It is essentially a tent on wheels, and its collapsible walls may be made of canvas, plastic, or fiberglass. At the other extreme are such land yachts as the Pegasus, a motor home that has two levels and in one version a maid's quarters on board—downstairs, of course. There are custom-designed coaches resplendent with chandeliers meant to cast a hospitable glow on the crystal and silver with which their owners are apt to entertain at dinner. Such glamour motor homes may have three air-conditioning systems, a trash compactor, an ice maker, a clothes washer and dryer, a central vacuum system, and a Jacuzzi. A coach customizer, appropriately named Magic Carpet Coaches, in Eugene, Oregon, installed a ten-thousand-dollar sound system in a Californian's forty-foot RV.

"It is so sophisticated," declared Bill Severs of Magic Carpet, "that it will self-adjust the sound level, up and down, to combat noise from outside."

The same vehicle has a TV system that allows its occupants to observe what is going on outside the vehicle both on the road and when parked. The owner of another land yacht scarcely has to worry about pulling a second vehicle along the highway, since a small sports car is tucked away in the bay.

A newcomer to the RV lifestyle may find the prospect of purchasing a first vehicle mind-boggling. Even veteran RVers discover that buying a new vehicle requires a great deal of thought and investigation. After all, the person who buys an RV is likely to spend more money on it than on any other purchase in a lifetime with the exception of a house or a college education for the children.

The Right RV for You

Before concentrating on the bewildering array of models, sizes, floor plans, and accessories that are available, you should ask yourself just how you are going to use the vehicle. Are you going to be on the road a good part of the year or for an annual vacation and perhaps a few weekends? How many people are to travel in the RV? Do you like to live close to nature, or would you prefer bringing along as many of the amenities of home as possible?

"For many would-be recreation vehicle owners, a frequent deterrent to their purchase of an RV is the fear they won't use their vehicle enough to get their money's worth," says Dr. Richard T. Curtin, who directed the University of Michigan study of the RV industry. "They have visions of their new RV rusting away in their driveway for all but the one week in the summer when they take it on their annual vacation." That does happen with some RV owners, but mostly because they have less free time than they expected—not because they discover they don't enjoy the lifestyle.

The University of Michigan study shows that such fears are in the main unfounded. The majority of RV families in the United States use their units more than just one week per year, and more than a quarter spend anywhere from a month to four months in their vehicles. The average works out to twenty-three days per year. To avoid impulse-buying errors, it is certainly a good idea to rent RVs of various types or borrow them from friends or relatives so that when you start talking to dealers, you will have some idea of the pluses and minuses of the various types and makes. This will give you a much better chance of purchasing an RV that suits your particular needs.

Doing Your Homework

The first thing to do is study the literature. Most likely your library or book store will have one or more of the annual RV buyers' guides. *Woodall's Buyer's Guide* (Woodall Publishing Company, 11 N. Skokie Highway, Lake Bluff, IL 60044) and *Trailer Life's Buyer's Guide* (TL Enterprises, Inc., 29901 Agoura Road, Agoura, CA 91301) are two such publications. These list the hundreds of RVs being offered and describe their principal features. You can also write to the Recreation Vehicle Industry Association (PO Box 2999, Reston, VA 22090, telephone 703-620-6003), or the Canadian Recreation Vehicle Association, 55 York Street, Suite 512, Toronto, Ontario, Canada, M5J 152 (416-362-8374) for information. (See Appendix B for RVIA's classification and description of RVs.) It is an even better idea to talk with friends and relatives who have experienced RV travel. They are invariably happy to describe their joys and triumphs and their travails as well. RVers don't mince words in discussing the short-comings and advantages of this make or that, of trailers versus campers or motor homes, and of installing various equipment such as a microwave oven, a TV, or an air conditioner.

Visit RV shows, which are advertised in local newspapers and held in major cities every year, usually

An RV Show

from midwinter to early spring, and look at the models currently available. Walk through the different vehicles on the heels of veteran RVers who, you soon learn, can look with the most jaundiced eye at what to your glance seems to be a superbly built and appointed pleasure palace on wheels. Find out about RV club meetings from RV dealers or, better yet, go to a campground in your own vicinity and chat with various RV campers who are spending the weekend there. They will most likely ply you with more coffee and other ready hospitality than you can easily endure, but they will also tell you about their unvarnished experiences with their rigs, past and present.

Choosing a Dealer

Only after you have done your homework should you go to a dealer. You will want to visit a number of dealers, but when you make your purchase, you should be sure that your dealer is entirely reliable.

"Pick a well-established dealer who's been in business for a reasonably long time, and who looks like he's going to stay in business," suggests Bob Ettleman, president of Motor Vacations Unlimited, one of the Midwest's largest dealers, in Elgin, Illinois. One veteran RVer also suggests that you look over the dealer's repair facilities to be sure the dealer's shop is large enough to repair the vehicles that it sells. And, finally, you want a dealer who is part of a national network of mechanics so that you can be certain of reliable repairs if your rig breaks down when you are traveling.

Let a dealer know that you are just looking over the possibilities, and don't let yourself fall prey to a hard sell. A dealer represents certain makes, of course, and you won't know how good they are until you've done a thorough job of looking over the field.

Questions to Answer Before Buying an RV

Do you plan to tow another vehicle or trailer with your RV? If so, will it be a small car, a four-wheel drive, a motorcycle, or a boat?

Would you feel comfortable driving a vehicle towing a trailer?

How many adults and children are likely to use the RV?

Do you plan to take the RV on weekend camp-outs or short vacation trips?

Do you prefer to tour long distances, or do you like to find a campground and stay there?

Do you intend to use the RV as a second car?

Do you like to camp in primitive campgrounds without hook-ups, or do you plan to camp as a rule in RV parks with all the facilities?

The Folding Camping Trailer

The folding camping trailer, or pop-up, is the least expensive RV. Its price may range from $1,500 to $8,000, but it also is possible to buy a used pop-up in good condition for as little as $250. It may also be known as a soft-top, pop-top, or fold-down, but whatever it is called, it provides the closest thing there is to tent camping. Pop-ups are popular. Better than one out of every hundred American families owns one. They range from simple trailers with a Coleman stove and space to lay down sleeping bags to campers that include water and electrical hookups and a boat rack atop. An elaborate pop-up includes not only a galley with a three-burner stove and a stainless steel sink and

A Pop-up, Open and Closed

refrigerator but also such amenities as a self-contained water tank, portable dining tables, ceiling lamps, and an electric furnace with electronic ignition. As a rule, a pop-up does not have a built-in toilet, but many pop-up campers bring along a portable chemical toilet. Many campers choose to use the facilities in the campground.

The weight and aerodynamic design of the pop-up are important, since, taken together, they determine how many miles per gallon you can cover with your tow vehicle and even whether your car should pull the trailer at all. A pop-up can be economical to tow if it is properly matched to the towing vehicle. A rule of thumb is that a car pulling a well-designed pop-up takes an extra gallon per every hundred miles. Look for one with a low trailer profile—this will save on gasoline, give greater stability, and cut down on the buffeting caused by passing trucks and crosswinds.

It is even more important to be sure that your car is hefty enough to pull a given pop-up or other trailer. Ordinarily a pop-up presents no problem, but some of the small autos simply do not have enough weight and horsepower to pull hardly anything. Rely *only* on the information regarding towing that the owner's manual of your automobile provides. Any other opinion is only guesswork.

One of the advantages of a pop-up is the short time it takes to set up. The mechanism that raises the top can do the job, often at the press of a button in ten to twenty seconds, but there are some pop-ups that have to be cranked slowly into erect position. When considering buying a pop-up, be sure to check that it has an easy-to-operate and trouble-free mechanism for raising the roof. Once a top has been raised, there must also be a safeguard against someone, usually a child, inadvertently lowering it and causing a tangle.

Inside a Pop-up

Pop-ups provide a great deal of sleeping space for their size; this makes them ideal for multiple-person use. Beds can slide out at each end or side of the trailer, and in most of the trailers, tables and seats convert into places to sleep at night. All told, pop-ups can sleep from four to six. Because they do not loom up behind the tow vehicle, pop-ups also are easy for the driver to see over and around. Even so, some states require that the tow vehicle have the same special rearview mirrors that are required to pull larger trailers. Certainly if the trailer being pulled is wider than the car, it is necessary to have mirrors that stick out far enough so that the driver can see around the trailer.

One thing is certain. A driver pulling a pop-up should never rely on a portable hitch. Most states require a permanent hitch, which can be installed by most RV dealers, and these are far safer. Select the hitch that the manufacturer of the towing vehicle specifies for the size and weight of the trailer you intend to pull. A safety chain should also connect the trailer to the car so that the chances of the trailer coming loose as the vehicle speeds down the interstate are eliminated. At the same time the correct electrical connections between car and trailer must be made so that the brakes, turn signals, and backup lights on the trailer can be activated by the driver.

Travel Trailers

A small travel trailer and a pop-up overlap in price, though it is hard to find a trailer that sells for less than $5,000, and you may have to pay $8,500 for one that has the accessories you want. One advantage is that a fifteen- to twenty-foot trailer (a small one) can be pulled by a subcompact car as well as by a larger auto, a small truck, or a four-wheel drive with the same ease that a pop-up can be pulled, and it requires the same type of trailer hitch. A trailer also can be easily disconnected from the tow vehicle, and it can be left in the campground just as readily as can a pop-up in case you want to drive off on an errand or go sightseeing in your car. A small travel trailer doesn't have the sleeping space of a pop-up, but it does provide such conveniences as a water heater, a refrigerator, an air conditioner, a toilet, and holding tanks. As inviting as these trailers may be, common sense and the laws of most states forbid people to ride in the trailer when it is being pulled.

In the next largest category of travel trailer are those that range from twenty to twenty-six feet in length, with a gross weight up to five thousand pounds,

A Travel Trailer

and are among the most popular RVs on the market. These medium-sized trailers are ideal for weekend travel but also are suitable for long trips or even full-time RV living. They are big enough to provide full bathroom facilities, a galley with sufficient counter space for any cook on wheels, and living, dining, and sleeping areas.

The advent of small cars on U.S. highways has cut into the popularity of the medium-sized travel trailer, since it weighs too much for such a car to pull. Larger family cars and pickups can tow such trailers, but the U.S. Department of Transportation urges that you be sure the braking system, suspension system, and tire and wheel combinations on the towing vehicle are matched to the type of trailer you are thinking of buying.

"A few inexperienced travel trailer users may hit the road with a 'make-do' tow vehicle such as an existing family car," comments Dave Tarrant, sales manager of Ford's recreation vehicle division. "But their vehicle is apt to lack the built-in components for han-

The Bathroom of a Travel Trailer

dling several tons of trailer loaded with food and gear for outdoor fun. As a result, their enjoyment of the wide-open spaces may be spoiled by problems ranging from extremely sluggish performance to expensive repairs on the road."

Tarrant also advises against underestimating the load a tow vehicle must handle. "Don't make the mistake of using only the published 'dry' weight of the empty trailer," he says. "You've got to consider the weight of food, dishes, cooking utensils, clothing, bedding, tools, hobby equipment—everything you put into it. Even water and propane add pounds.''

Before buying a trailer, you must match its estimated weight against the capacity of the car or truck with which you plan to pull it. One way to arrive at an accurate estimate is to ask your RV dealer for the trailer's Gross Vehicle Weight Rating. The GVWR indicates the maximum weight of a fully loaded trailer, based on the manufacturer's research.

Trailers have their advantages over other kinds of RVs. They include all the comforts of home and are as self-contained as any motor homes. After you have set up your rig at a camp, you can use the towing vehicle for errands and sightseeing. And, since a trailer does not have an engine, it depreciates slowly, which makes

A Luxurious RV Living Room

it a good investment—if you decide to resell it.

On the other hand, it takes a powerful truck or car to pull all but the smallest trailer, and a trailer cuts gas mileage down substantially, depending, of course, on its size, weight, and amount of wind resistance. On the road its length can be a problem both when you pass a slower vehicle and when someone else passes you. It also takes practice before you learn the knack of backing it into a camping site. Campers with a trailer fully appreciate a campground that has pull-through spaces, where all you have to do is pull in, unhook, and when you get ready to leave, hook up and pull right out the other side.

Everything that is true of the medium-sized trailer is even more so of the enormous trailers that run up to thirty-five feet, a length established in many states as the longest allowed on the road. These trailers are preferred by people who are going to spend much or all of their time living in them. They are every bit as luxurious and comfortable as the top-of-the-line motor homes, but weighing as they do up to ten thousand pounds, they require tow vehicles capable of moving such an enormous weight safely and without breakdowns.

Fifth Wheelers

The fifth-wheel trailer has found a ready market in recent years. Descended from the 1932 Curtis Aerocar, which featured a raised bubble at the front so that its occupants could look over the roof of the tow vehicle, the fifth wheeler usually has dual tires in the rear to make up four wheels, with the pickup truck providing the fifth wheel. Since the fifth wheeler's hitch rests on a pickup's bed, this RV handles very easily on the road

A Fifth-Wheel Travel Trailer

and is simple to back into a campsite. Its fixed pivot point makes the fifth wheeler far more maneuverable than other trailers. At least twenty-nine states also allow passengers to ride inside a fifth-wheel trailer, since its hitch is not likely to come undone, and it has more safety and stability on the road than do other trailers. The fifth wheeler is also more commodious than other trailers of comparable length because the raised section over the hitch makes possible a bedroom large enough for twin beds or a queen-sized bed complete with bedside tables.

Truck Campers

The Recreation Vehicle Industry Association (RVIA) also classifies a truck camper as a variety of trailer, but it actually is a camping unit that is affixed to the bed or chassis of a truck. It may simply provide space for a couple of mattresses and a Coleman stove, or it may contain an electric or gas refrigerator, water tanks with sink and pump, toilets, double and single beds, and hookups for electricity and water. The truck camper,

A Truck Camper

especially when mounted on a four-wheel drive, is outstanding for rough roads, and it is easy to take the entire vehicle with you or go to the trouble of jacking the camper off the truck bed in order to leave it at the campsite. Most truck campers have plenty of power and can carry a moped or bike without difficulty or pull a small car or dune buggy.

Van Conversions

Some families find a van conversion the most practical RV for their way of life. Van conversions are economical to operate and can serve many purposes. The

RVIA defines a van conversion as a completed van chassis modified esthetically or decoratively in appearance by the RV manufacturer for transportation and recreational purposes. These changes may include windows, carpeting, paneling, seats, sofas, and accessories.

There are also van campers to which have been added sleeping, kitchen, and toilet facilities, 110-volt hookup, fresh water storage, water hookup, and sometimes a top extension to provide more head room. Vans can pull a boat or a trailer while providing solid comfort; they also can serve as a second car, since they can negotiate city streets or narrow roads with a great deal more agility than can a conventional motor home. They are easy to park, and the mini vans are even garageable. As a result, many van owners use them for travel, for commuting to work, or for transporting the family to community happenings. They are fine for tailgate parties or camping trips.

A Van Conversion

Motor Homes

Today motor homes compete in luxury with the most lavish of the trailers. These self-powered RVs provide living facilities both on the road and in camp. Some motor homes are built on a metal bed extending behind a truck engine and resemble a bus; others are built directly on a heavy-duty truck chassis, with a bed up over the cab. They are usually eight feet wide and range from twenty to thirty-five feet in length. Designed and built by the RV manufacturers, they offer a bewildering variety with dozens of options. Since they are directly accessible from the driver's seat, they are particularly convenient for on-the-road use of their facilities. Their expanding popularity can only be matched by their prices, which might run anywhere from $15,000 to $300,000.

Motor home owners value the ease with which they can start off on a camping trip. All they need to

A Mini Motor Home

The Sleeping Area of a Motor Home

do is load the vehicle, and they are ready to go. There
is no hitching up the trailer. Arriving in a campground
is just as simple. They pull into the site, check that the
vehicle is level so the refrigerator will function properly, and plug in. The only disadvantage is that motor
homes have to go where their owners go unless they
tow a second vehicle behind them. Since a sturdy RV
can pull such disparate things as a small four-wheel
drive, a compact car, a horse van, a trailer with a rac-
ing car aboard, or a trailer carrying a boat, this need
not present much of a problem. It remains that to tow
a second vehicle or trailer not only lowers the gas mileage, which in any large motor home is not very good in
the first place, but for most people also adds to the
strain of driving. The same fuel-economy measures
available in automobiles can be expected in RVs. Such
improvements in automatic transmissions as lockup or

split torque converters and overdrive can also be found in RVs.

RVs for Travelers with Disabilities

People with disabilities can be enthusiastic RVers, but only with a vehicle that provides ready access from the driver's seat to the living quarters. This usually means that a motor home is most appropriate for them, though a van can also be modified to include a flush toilet, a bed, and a wheelchair lift. Although a disabled RVer can save money by buying a used RV, the vehicle then must be modified. As a rule, the door must be widened and a wheelchair lift installed. Other important changes include the installation of hand controls and the removal of built-in furniture and fixtures that otherwise might impede the free movement of a wheelchair within the vehicle. A wheelchair-level sink and convenient toilet facilities can also be put in.

Disabled people who buy a new RV should have the necessary modifications made at the factory. The Recreation Vehicle Industry Association can provide a list of RV manufacturers that specialize in making vehicles that are suitably modified for the disabled.

For more information on RVs for travelers with disabilities, write to Handicapped Travel Club, Inc., 667 J Avenue, Coronado, CA 91118, 619-435-5213.

Looking for Quality

Regardless of what kind of RV you decide to buy, you should pay strict attention to its construction and the R-value of its insulation against heat and cold and road noises. Before buying an RV, don't be shy about looking into cabinets, under beds, and even under the floor to get a good idea of how well constructed the vehicle is. An RV should be practical to live in, too, and you might well take into consideration how easy it is to make up the beds or take a shower. (One woman discovered that the only way she could take a shower in her rig was to stand on top of the toilet!) Check out details of plumbing and electrical wiring as well as accessibility of such equipment as the furnace, the water pump, and the water lines for ease of maintenance. It is important, too, to know whether the RV you are considering has roll bars, which are supports that keep the roof from collapsing in case of a crash. In order to make an RV as light and economical to drive as possible, some manufacturers have eliminated roll bars and contented themselves with wood instead of steel tubular framing.

One way you can be reasonably assured of quality construction in an RV is to look for the oval seal that the RVIA requires of its member manufacturers, who must build their units to meet the fire, safety, plumbing, electrical, and LP-gas systems standards approved by the American National Standards Institute for RVs. Members of the RVIA not only must live up to more than 450 specifications but also are subject to spot inspections without notice.

You can get a first-hand impression of how well a given RV is built by visiting the plant. My wife and I have visited several RV plants, and once we watched our actual RV being constructed. It was reassuring to watch competent workmen, descendants of Hoosier wagon makers, at work. On the other hand, we've watched lackadaisical workers in another plant putting together vehicles that—when slicked up with cabinets, carpeting, and furniture—could easily pass superficial inspection.

Experienced RVers are exacting in their survey of a vehicle they are considering purchasing. They are interested in everything from its aerodynamic front, designed to reduce drag; the tinted windshield, to reduce glare; the undercoating, to prevent rusting; the double entry step, to make entry and exit easier; and the deadbolt lock for the entry door, to increase security. How much interior and exterior storage is there? Do the drawers slide easily, or do they catch? Are the drawers and cabinet doors fitted with latches that will not come undone when the vehicle takes a sudden twist on the road or hits a bump? What kinds of windows does the rig have? What size water tank is aboard? Are the hot- and cold-water lines located so that they can easily be emptied for cold-weather storage? The list of questions can seem endless, but these are all things that should be considered.

Shopping for Price

Once you've decided which RV suits your travel recreation plans best, you can start shopping for price. An RV can usually be bought for less than the manufacturer's list price, and it is worthwhile to look up the RV of your choice in one of the RV "blue books" available at most libraries and some banks. You'll find figures for both new and used RVs in the book; these should give you a good idea of what sort of deal you may eventually be able to obtain. Above all, do not buy an RV without taking it out for a test drive. Many dealers will rent you a vehicle for a test weekend, which is even better; some will even apply the weekend's rental against the purchase price in case you decide to buy.

Many RV campers begin with pop-ups or small

trailers and then after a few years come down with what is known as trade-up fever. Once again they start eyeing trailers, fifth-wheelers, and motor homes with covetous eyes. Trade-up fever strikes without warning and with equal intensity every few years. RV travelers are always looking for ways to improve their mobile abodes. As a result, there are plenty of good buys in used RVs around, and these are well worth a first-time RV buyer's consideration.

Building Your Own RV

You may decide to build your own RV. Every year tens of thousands of people convert vans to RV use, and some do-it-yourselfers convert old school buses and trucks into rigs that may be furnished with antiques, employ a wood-burning stove, or run on methane or propane instead of gasoline. One couple remodeled a log truck with its ten wheels, fifteen gears, and thundering engine into one of the most redoubtable RVs in the Pacific Northwest. U.S. campgrounds are home to some wild and wonderful contraptions as well as the commercially built RVs that most people prefer.

4
Financing and Insurance

"A recreation vehicle depreciates like a boat, and not like a car," says David Humphreys, president of the Recreation Vehicle Industry Association. "Therefore lenders will lend money for longer terms on RVs than on cars."

According to Humphreys, loans of seven to ten years on new RVs are typical. A loan on a used RV is more likely to span from five to seven years. A study released in 1986 by Jon Whitney Associates, of Austin, Texas, of 319 banks, credit unions, finance firms, and savings and loan associations at 8,123 locations throughout the United States ascertained that 60 to 84 months was typical of the length of maturity for direct RV consumer loans. Indirect loans made through RV dealers reached maturity between 84 and 120 months, which Robert Rawlings, vice president of CIT Financial Services, believes provide RV buyers with more manageable monthly payments. Such lengthy maturity periods are made possible by the low RV delinquency rate, which in 1985 reached 1.73 percent, according to the American Bankers Association.

Arranging Credit

"RV buyers are reliable buyers," states Rawlings. "They enjoy their RVs and don't want to risk losing them."

This is a big plus when you start arranging a loan, since financial institutions that have had experience with RV buyers know that RV owners will give up a lot before they will give up their RVs. RV buyers are what financial and marketing people call upscale and are not likely to default. Even if they did fail to make payments and the vehicle had to be repossessed, it could easily be sold at close to its original purchase price, which is the reverse of what happens to a repossessed automobile.

According to the Survey Research Center of the University of Michigan, half of all new RVs purchased are bought on time. Thirty percent of used vehicles other than RVs are bought on time. Younger buyers are likely to take out a loan simply because they already have commitments to such things as home mortgages and children's educations, which tie up ready cash. The older RV buyers also are likely to buy on time because they may well have their assets tied up in long-term savings plans or investments.

Usually a down payment of 15 to 25 percent is required, but sapient buyers make as large a down payment as they can, commensurate with their other financial considerations. This cuts down on monthly payments. They also insist upon a provision in their contract that will allow them to pay off the loan with no penalty in advance of its maturation date to minimize the amount of interest they must pay. They choose a maturation period as short as is practicable so that they minimize their interest payments in this way as well.

Shopping for a Loan

It is also important to shop around for a loan. You may obtain a loan through a commercial bank, a savings and loan association, a credit union, or a finance company; you may also borrow against your paid-up life insurance policy. Your insurance agent can tell you whether this is a practical possibility for you. An advantage of borrowing against your life insurance is that you will not have to make monthly payments providing the cash value of your policy is large enough to meet annual interest payments. If you are unfortunate enough to die with the loan still outstanding, the sum owed will be subtracted from the face value of your policy.

In shopping for a lower rate of interest, it is valuable to employ collateral such as stocks or bonds, a bank savings account, or perhaps a second mortgage on your home. It is also valuable to seek a loan where you already have ongoing financial relations, since you will have established a good credit rating.

Most RV dealers are more than happy to assist you in obtaining an indirect loan. The dealer goes to a bank and presumably obtains the lowest possible interest rate. Dealers add on a certain percentage to arrange the financing, and it is critical to know whether you or the bank are paying this extra amount.

"A dealer may give you a super deal on the unit and make up the money on the banking package," points out Bob Ettleman of Motor Vacations Unlimited.

It is also critical to examine whether you are to pay simple or compound interest. Dealers usually can arrange for you to make a lower down payment if they arrange the financing, but this is not necessarily to your advantage. They should be able to obtain a prevailing lending rate for you, and in some cases they may even be willing to assume some of the liability in case you should default.

Lending Institutions

A commercial bank, a credit union, or a savings and loan association places a lien against your RV when it gives you a direct or indirect loan. A lien sounds unsettling, but most people who have purchased a house have already learned to live with the prospect, no matter how remote, that their dwelling might be taken away from them if they do not keep up their payments. At least one advantage of a conventional loan is that if you default because of health or business problems, only your motor home can be taken away from you. Once you apply for your loan, it usually takes only a few days to be approved, though it is a good idea to seek approval from a lending institution before you make your purchase.

Some RV buyers think it is appropriate that they should take out a second mortgage on their home to pay for their "home on wheels." If you borrow against the equity in your home, you can usually obtain the lowest rate of interest possible as well as longer terms. Among the disadvantages is that the loan may take several weeks to be approved, and if you do indeed fail to keep up your payments, you would be endangering not only your RV but your home as well.

Avoiding Pitfalls

As in arranging loans for any other purpose, there are pitfalls to avoid. It is important to read the agreements carefully, small print and all. It is also a good idea to avoid the dangerous finance plans proposed by a few dealers. In their eagerness to sell a vehicle to you, they may offer a deal that requires practically nothing down and low monthly payments for perhaps three years, when you are expected to make an enormous balloon payment.

"You'll have no difficulty in financing the balloon payment when the time comes," the dealer may say, but usually when the time comes, there is indeed difficulty, and you either have to come up with the payment or have your RV repossessed.

Another plan that many dealers offer is the lease back. The dealer sells you the RV, and the dealer leases it back from you for a period of six months to three years. Then he rents out the unit when you are not using it yourself and shares the income with you on a fifty/fifty basis. Your share can be applied against your monthly payments. Since the dealer provides maintenance and storage for your vehicle, this may be a good deal if you only want to use the vehicle yourself for a few weeks every year. However, many experienced RVers warn that this is an oversold concept and that when there are too many rigs available for rent in a given area, your chances of coming out well are at best unpredictable.

Sometimes several buyers join together to buy an RV and share the use of it on an agreed-upon schedule.

"Anybody can time-share," cautions Ralph Smith, chief of the state of Washington's Department of Licensing. "They can put a dollar down and go out and make all kinds of promises and take a lot of people's money. Without financial resources and a valid financial plan, though, the buyer is only getting an illusion." There may indeed be valid time-share offers, but it is a good idea to look at them with a jaundiced eye.

Until recently, RV manufacturers were not providing finance incentives to help their dealers sell their vehicles, but in 1986 a number of the manufacturers undertook to make possible financing at lower rates of interest than otherwise could be obtained. So far these offers have been made for limited times only through selected dealers and require customers to meet down payment and credit requirements.

Insuring an RV

Dealers are ready not only to help with financing a purchase but also to arrange the insurance. Most likely the place for you to start in making certain that your RV is fully covered is the agent who has written your existing auto and homeowner's policies. (AARP members may obtain RV as well as auto insurance through the AARP.) You may have to obtain a separate policy for your RV, or you may be able to have riders added to your existing policy.

As in buying auto insurance, your RV insurance rates are going to vary depending on your exact coverage, your driving record, your state, and whether your RV is driven or towed. You may discover that your existing auto policy covers tent trailers or travel trailers that you may tow, but it may be necessary to have a rider added. Be sure that your insurance covers the trailer both on the road and when parked.

Policies can include collision benefits, emergency living expenses, and towing. Your motor home should be covered against the aforementioned risks; in addition, you will want coverage similar to what you require to drive an auto. This includes coverage for personal liability, bodily injury, property damage, medical payments, uninsured motorists, and collision.

Even if you are only renting an RV, you should be certain that your own existing auto policy or the dealer's policy will cover you in all respects. Conversely, if you rent your RV to someone else, be sure that the vehicle is covered against both damage and personal liability.

Several of the recreation vehicle clubs offer insurance packages to their members. If you are already a member of a club, you should inquire about the club's insurance program. You even may want to join a particular RV club if you learn that it has significant cost-saving insurance benefits or that it covers rescue assistance or medical evacuation.

5
Renting an RV

The spring rains had carpeted the southwestern desert with flowers, and if Joan, my wife, was going to photograph them in all their ephemeral beauty, there was no time to lose. We flew to Los Angeles, where we were met at the airport and driven to Palm Springs. A rented motor home awaited us at the Thousand Trails Resort Campground. There was no need to bring along bed linens and blankets or a housekeeping kit because it could all be rented too. Aside from no lids for the cooking pots, and no fly swatter, everything else, including a pair of wineglasses, was already in the rig.

It did not take us long to drive to the Joshua Tree National Monument, only forty or so miles away, where the flowers were in full bloom. From there it was an easy cruise in our rented motor home to the Saguaro National Monument in Arizona, where the flowering season was also still at its height.

A Rig in Joshua Tree National Monument in California

Fly-and-Drive an RV

For RV travelers who want to get to the area that they wish to visit in a hurry, a fly-and-rent-an-RV package is the way to go. Air Canada, Eastern, and Northwest Orient have pioneered in packaging air-and-RV vacations in the United States and Canada, and other carriers are expected to enter the field in the next year or so. Amtrak and a national RV rental agency also offer a rail–motor home vacation. Then, too, unusual RV vacation opportunities are provided by such concerns as Baja Adventures of Encino, California, which not only takes tourists in rented RVs to Mexico but also is now offering summer Alaska motor home adventures. These include air transportation and fares for the RV and its passengers aboard the Sundance Cruises' flagship, the *M.V. Stardancer*, from Vancouver to Alaska, and the Alaska Marine Ferry from Haines to Juneau. A wagon master guide leads the twenty-four-foot RVs on a tour over Alaskan highways.

Interest in and opportunities for RV rental vacations are growing phenomenally, and vacationers with limited time are finding it convenient to jet across the country so that they can then slow down to a camper's leisured pace. They find it easy to call up a travel agent or an airline and make arrangements. Some of the fly-and-drive-an-RV plans even include discounts in the air fares and motor home rentals or provide free mileage for a day or two on the road.

Trying Out an RV

Another popular motive for renting an RV for a weekend, a week, or longer is to try it out. People who are considering purchasing a certain type of motor home or trailer rent them first to see whether they really enjoy RV travel and whether they like that particular vehicle. For this reason many RV dealers offer rentals with the hope that the rentals will lead to sales. Some even offer to apply the rental fees against the purchase price if a prospective RVer decides to buy. Sometimes they have a good number of years to wait for the purchase, since many families who enjoy RV travel also are in no hurry to buy. Renting may be the common-sense approach if they are only going to take a trip or two a year.

RV rentals have turned into big business. A University of Michigan Survey Research Center sampling of 3,900 consumers in 1986 revealed that 20.8 percent of the respondents were planning to rent an RV within the next twelve months. There was, in fact, a stronger preference for renting over buying an RV.

"Motor home rentals today are where car rentals were twenty years ago," says Robert A. Smalley, president of American Land Cruisers, one of the leading national RV rental companies.

Renting a motor home or a trailer calls for a bit of planning. You should choose the vehicle that fits your own plans. With RVs of all kinds available for rent, you can pick anything from a simple pop-up trailer to a resplendent motor home. A folding camping trailer not only costs much less to rent than any other type of RV, but it also might be just the thing for a camp in the woods where you plan to hike and fish. On the other hand, a luxurious motor home might be ideal for a base at a football game. Hundreds of Chicagoans who could not get into the New Orleans hotels crowded with luckier football fans during the 1986 Super Bowl contest rented RVs in Chicago and drove to Louisiana, where they were able to park them in campgrounds within easy driving distance of the stadium. Other people rent RVs for reasons as dissimilar as touring New England's forests to observe the fall foliage and going skiing in the Rockies.

It may not be quite so critical to choose a dependable place to rent an RV as it is to choose a reliable dealer to buy from, but it is important enough. After all, who wants the rented vehicle to fall apart on the road and spoil your vacation? You may simply look in the Yellow Pages under Recreational Vehicles for dealers who rent RVs, but this does not give you any idea of whether the dealer is reliable. Choose a dealer who has given satisfactory service to a trusted friend or relative.

Another source of rental information is *Who's Who in RV Rentals,* a directory published by the Recreation Vehicle Rental Association (RVRA), which includes information on rental services and prices and is available for four dollars through RVRA, 3251 Old Lee Highway, Fairfax, VA 22030. The book also describes the type and length of the RVs available, how many each one sleeps, the rental fees, and the minimum number of rental days required. Most people who rent RVs plan to return them where they checked them out, but others want to take them to another city, and it is important to learn exactly how much more such an option will cost. There are even one-way coast-to-coast plans available; these vary in price from a small charge to several hundred dollars, depending upon whether the rental company wishes to move vehicles from one area to another.

RV rental costs run about as follows according to the Recreation Vehicle Dealers Association: for a big motor home, $500 to $800 a week; folding camping trailer, $130 to $225 a week; mini motor home, $275 to $500; travel trailer, $130 to $400. Mileage is also charged, and these charges vary considerably, so readers should balance out what may seem a lower rental fee for a given RV against the mileage charges.

There are several national RV rental sources, including U-Haul International, the largest renter of hitches and trailers, which has entered the RV rental field. (See Appendix A for addresses and telephone numbers of places to contact for listings of RV sources in your area.)

Choosing the Right RV

You are likely to have a negative experience about RV travel if you rent too small a vehicle. Do not believe glib assertions as to how many people a given RV will sleep. Some rental people will claim that a vehicle sleeps six, and theoretically this may be true, but only if two are very small children who do not mind bunking together on a lumpy, jerry-built bed assembled nightly from what during the day is a dining table. It is a good idea to match the number of people the vehicle can accommodate during the day with the number it can sleep. The extra amount it may cost you to rent a somewhat larger RV will turn out to be well worth spending.

If you have never driven an RV, it is important to have the rental agent instruct you carefully and take you out on a test drive before you sign the contract. Almost all RVs have automatic transmission, and it is not difficult for a neophyte to get the hang of cruising down the road at the helm of a vacation home on wheels, but a test drive should be mandatory. It is also important to have the agent demonstrate all the equipment of the RV so that you know how everything from the generator to the microwave oven operates. You will want to know how to hook up your plumbing, fresh water, and electrical connections in campgrounds and where you put gasoline into the vehicle. I remember with amusement the RV renter who pulled into a gas station to fill up and then searched wildly around for the gas tank, which turned out not to be on the side of the rig he had so laboriously snuggled up close to the pumps. You should also go over the interior and exterior of the RV to be sure that the agent notes everything from a cigarette burn in a couch to a dent in the rear bumper. You do not want to run the risk of having to pay for a previous renter's mistakes.

RV renters have to make essentially the same choices as do RV buyers when considering whether they want a trailer or a motor home. Renting a motor home means that once you are in a campground, you do not have a handy vehicle to use to run into town on an errand or go on a side trip. You may want to pull a small car. If so, be sure that your contract allows you to do so. Many rental agencies do not permit towing with their motor homes, since towing a trailer or second vehicle can damage the transmission of the RV. You may be able to bring along a bicycle or moped that can be stored inside the RV or attached to it to provide supplementary transportation, at least in the campground.

If you decide in favor of a trailer, be sure that the agreement includes the connections between your car and the trailer and the trailer license. Some trailer rental agencies require that you bring your own hitch or buy one from them. If the hitch is part of the deal, do not accept a bumper hitch. It is much safer to have your hitch connected directly to the frame of the car. In most states bumper hitches are illegal.

Selecting a Rental Dealer

Since RV rentals vary a great deal from one agency to another, you should shop around. Probably the best thing to do is first talk with friends and relatives who have rented RVs themselves and find out what sort of service they had from the company they chose. It is a good idea to rent an RV in the less busy months, from September 15 to May 15, if at all possible because you can then take advantage of off-season rates. At least make your reservations early so that you do not have to accept any rate that a rental agency offers you in order to have an RV when everybody else seems to be asking for one too.

When you are shopping for an RV rental, find out whether the dealer charges extra for such things as propane and toilet chemicals or whether they are part of the package price. Most dealers do require a damage deposit, which varies but amounts to a few hundred dollars. This sum must be paid in advance, but the money will be refunded to you if you return the vehicle without any damage and in clean interior condition.

It is one of the irksome but understandable conditions of renting an RV that most dealers expect you to pay for everything in advance. This includes the deposit, the rental fee, and in many cases even an estimated mileage fee. Of course, the unused portion of this mileage fee will be returned to you when you bring the vehicle back. You also must pay for the gasoline your rented RV requires, and this can be an important part of your costs if you decide to drive long distances. If you use a credit card, most dealers will at least forgo the estimated mileage fee.

Insurance is something to keep in mind when you rent an RV. The rental fee usually includes collision and liability insurance, but there is often a deductible running as high as five hundred dollars. You may prefer to check your own auto insurance policy to see whether you would be covered in case of accident; still it may be a good idea to buy a collision damage waiver covering the deductible and have peace of mind on your trip.

Be sure that your contract covers any breakdowns on the trip. You may be entitled to a rental car while your rented rig is being fixed, and a refund should be made for every day you cannot use the RV. Since reputable rental agencies keep their rigs in good condition and generally retire them from rental service after sixty-thousand miles or so, you are not likely to encounter trouble; but there are glitches in any machine, and an RV, with its complicated systems, is very much a machine. Some national RV rental agencies have twenty-four-hour road service, and all you need to do is call a toll-free 800 number in case you have problems on the road. This is one good reason to be careful about renting an RV from an individual. You undoubtedly can get a much lower price from a person who advertises in the want ads or who happens to live just down the street, but can you be sure that the vehicle is in good condition? Also, what happens if you break down several hundred miles from home and you rented the RV from a neighbor who, even if well-meaning, has no means of helping you out of your troubles?

Some people who rent RVs allow themselves to be pushed around by dealers. A dealer may claim that a vehicle will only be available on certain days of the week. Dealers should not be allowed to tailor your vacation plans to their convenience. It also is usually possible to pick up the vehicle the evening before your trip begins so that you can load it. The dealer as a rule does not charge you for an extra day, though there may be an added insurance premium so that you are covered on that evening as well.

Most people who rent RVs intend to travel in them, but some enjoy staying in an RV with no intention of moving it from where they find it moored.

"I enjoy being in my rented trailer, but I don't want to pull it anywhere," explained a woman we met at Fort Wilderness Campground at the Walt Disney World Resort, part of Disney World in Florida. Fort Wilderness rents trailers with maid service to visitors who prefer to stay in them instead of a hotel. Some campground resorts also rent trailers to vacationers who have no desire to travel in an RV. They simply want to enjoy the amenities of the resort.

"Perhaps some day I'll want to take a trip in an RV," added the lady at Fort Wilderness. "Now I'm just getting the hang of living in it."

6
Planning a Trip

A happy RV camping trip does not begin in the leafy forests of Maine or the Sierra high country of California. It begins at home.

Checking the Literature

Put the books, brochures, and maps you have gathered on the kitchen table and let everyone going consider the alternatives. Camping facilities can be found at national monuments; in national parks, national forests, Army Corps of Engineers recreation areas, Bureau of Land Management public lands, and state, county, and municipal parks and forests; on some Indian reservations; at Tennessee Valley Authority sites in the Middle South; and across the border, in Canadian national, provincial, and local parks and Crown lands. Campers are also welcome at private campgrounds, and these range from places to park your rig for the night to resort campgrounds. (See Appendix C for a map of the United States showing the main tourist sites and Appendix D for a listing of federal campground offices, campground chains, camp resort organizations, campground directories, and appropriate addresses where you may obtain additional information for planning your trip.)

Write for booklets and other information to the states or Canadian provinces that you plan to visit. Many of these states and provinces also provide free highway maps. You can also send a self-addressed, stamped, business-sized envelope to the National Campground Owners Association, 804 D Street, NW, Washington, DC 20002, for a list of private campgrounds in any state. Perhaps you already have a travel guidebook that lists the addresses of the various state or province tourist organizations, or this information may be available in your public library. Some veteran RVers simply do this: they address their request to a state's department of tourism in the state capital and include, of course, the state and zip code. If, for example, they were seeking information on South Dakota, they would write to the South Dakota Department of Tourism, Pierre, South Dakota 57501. Your local post office can give you the zip code for any city in the country, and you can find the state capital in your road atlas if you happen to have forgotten it. In response you will receive brochures, maps, and sometimes discount coupons to some of the attractions. Allow at least six weeks for a reply, particularly if you are getting close to the busy summer travel season.

Since the national parks of the United States are among the top RV travel destinations, chances are that you will find literature provided by the park service to be particularly valuable in making your plans. Write to the Office of Public Inquiries, National Park Service, Washington, DC 20240, and ask for the foldout brochure titled, *Guide and Map—National Parks of the United States.* The brochure shows the locations of all U.S. national parks and includes addresses and other information for each park. While you are at it, ask also for *Camping in the National Park System.* There is no charge for either publication. You can also write to the Recreation Vehicle Industry Association, PO Box 2999, Department POF, Reston, VA 22090, and ask for the free catalog that describes more than twenty-five camping publications. You should include a business-sized, stamped, self-addressed envelope. If you place an order from outside the United States, you should include a bank draft in U.S. funds for the amount of one dollar to cover air mail return postage.

Avoiding Crowds

The park service suggests that you try the newer, lesser known parks and monuments, particularly during the peak months of June, July, and August, when schools are closed and families are vacationing with their youngsters. You might also do well to plan your trips in April and May or September and October, when the parks are less crowded. In April 1986, my wife and I visited Grand Canyon National Park, one of the most popular of all the parks, and had no trouble at all in putting our RV into the campground. During the busiest part of the summer, it is almost impossible to find a site there. Also we were able to tour the canyon rim in our RV, stopping at scenic overlooks and easily finding a parking place at each spot. At the height of the season, RVs are not even allowed to tour the rim because of traffic congestion.

It is also a good idea to make advance reservations if you plan to take raft or pack trips when you are in a national park. Most of these in-park activities are operated by private companies under contract to the National Park Service. The Conference of National Park Visitor Facilities and Services (c/o Mr. G. B. Hanson, National Park Concessions, Inc., Mammoth Cave, KY 42259) will send you a copy of a book titled *National Park Visitor Facilities and Services* if you send $4.05. If you live abroad, you must send $6.05 in U.S. funds.

You certainly will want a current road atlas and an up-to-date campground guide. These are available in bookstores. If you have a particular hobby, such as antique collecting or getting to know American Indians better, you probably will want specialized guidebooks and other in-depth publications that will come in handy as you make your plans. Membership in the Good Sam Club or the Family Motor Coach Association is invaluable to families planning RV trips.

Discover Your Own Backyard

One other suggestion should help make your trip a successful one, particularly if it is your first experience in an RV: discover your own backyard. Wherever you live, there are fascinating things to see and do only a short drive away. If you have a weekend to spend, there is little point in driving a considerable distance when there are enjoyable things close at hand.

Doubtless you can climb into a motor home or a vehicle pulling a trailer for the first time and set off on a lengthy vacation with impunity, but it stands to reason that if you can possibly do so, you should first try some weekend trips near home. You can work out the bugs in the rig and get used to RV living close to home, where you can talk to the dealer about any problems that may arise.

Think of the things you like to do. A man is an ardent bird-watcher and swimmer, his wife a fisherwoman and rockhound. This family might be able to find a place where all their interests can be satisfied at one time. Most likely they will have to make an agreement. On this trip, they will do some of their favorite things; on the next trip, they will do other things.

What to Take Along

Once you know where you are going and what you plan to do, a list of items to take along is in order. Consider the activities that you have in mind, the weather, and the characteristics of the countryside where you are going to journey. You may be traveling in a commodious RV instead of the family car, but this does not mean that you can take along all the paraphernalia that you are used to at home. Keep things relatively simple.

"Be plain in the woods," said Horace Kephart, the veteran camper, who around the turn of the century wrote about camping in his book *Camping and Woodcraft*. "We seek the woods to escape civilization for a time and all that suggests it. It is one of the blessings of wilderness life that it shows us how few things we need to be perfectly happy."

Some RV campers whom you are likely to encounter in the nation's campgrounds would profit from Kephart's admonition. They complicate their travel with so many encumbrances that they spend much of their time in maintenance.

Good eating in your RV begins at home too. Plan the menus together and make up your initial shopping list. Part of the fun of RV travel is shopping along the road and in the towns you pass through, but you should bring the staples from home.

Camping Safety

RV camping safety begins at home as well. You should put together a first-aid kit (see below) that will meet your emergency needs both on the road and in camp, and if you plan to go boondocking to remote areas, at least one of the adults going on the trip should take the American Red Cross first-aid course.

First-Aid Kit for Your RV

6 elastic bandages, three to four inches wide
4 instant ice packs
set of seventeen-inch splints
set of thirty-inch splints
two-inch roller bandage
2 one-inch roller bandages
6 three-by-three-inch sterile pads
6 four-by-four-inch sterile pads
large box of assorted adhesive bandages
24 alcohol swabs
scissors
tweezers
safety pins

How to Read a Road Map

Knowing how to read a road map is a key to safer driving; it also can save money and traffic frustration. A map can tell a skilled driver when it is more economical and practical to strike across country on secondary roads and when it would be wisest to follow the interstates. Terrain and city traffic, as well as distances, influence driving times and costs. Off the interstates it is often possible to locate outstanding restaurants in case you decide to "eat out" and quieter campgrounds that are less expensive than those along the main roads.

Reading a road map is not as difficult as folding it. If you play the accordion, you have the edge on all other RVers when it comes to folding a road map. Although crumpled and rumpled from being passed from pilot to navigator and back, a map will return easily to its original neat package if you open it to its fullest and fold it exactly as if you were playing a squeeze box. This piece of information is bound to be cheerful news to RV travelers, many of whom would just as soon wrestle a python in their moving vehicle than attempt to refold a road map while traveling.

Highway maps usually show such familiar things as routes, mileage, and driving time between cities and also indicate recreation areas, camping sites, boat launching ramps, and points of interest. A good source of road maps is *Rand McNally Road Atlas* (available in bookstores and at newsstands).

Five tips on reading a road map are given below.

1. Study the legend for an explanation of map markings and symbols.

2. Compute mileage by totaling the figures shown alongside the highway route, or look up the mileage between key cities if your road atlas has such a table. Some RVers prefer to lay a piece of paper along the route and make pencil marks on the edge of it for each section of road. The distance from the first mark to the last will indicate the distance to be dri-

Explanation of Symbols

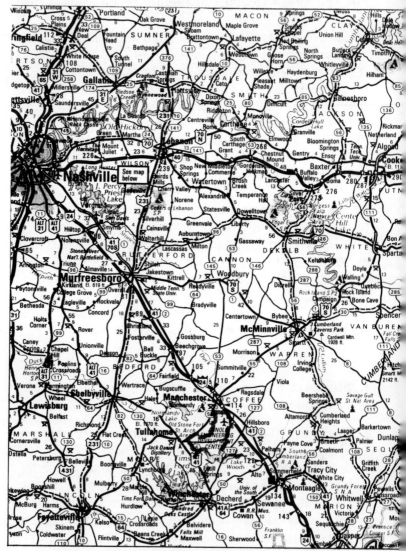

🏕 State Parks (with camping facilities)

⛺ State Parks (without camping facilities)

✗ Waysides, Roadside Parks

▲ Campsites

✈ Airports

■ Points of Interest

▲▼ Service Areas

⬓ Rest Areas

S.P. State Parks

S.F. State Forests

S.R. State Reserves

Free Limited–Access Highways

Toll Limited–Access Highways

Other Four-Lane Divided Highways

Principal Highways

Other Through Highways

Other Roads

Unpaved Roads

Scenic Routes

If you familiarize yourself with the map's legend, you will be able to make the fullest use of your road maps.

ven. The total number of miles can be measured by holding the marked paper up to the scale of miles in the legend.

3. Use the specialty map inserts on the state maps. Large-scale maps of cities and metropolitan areas and complicated interstate interchanges can be studied in advance to plan a route through or around a city that will save time and prevent ruffled tempers. If you know that a mile down the expressway you are going to have to exit to the left, you can get into a left lane in plenty of time to avoid last-minute lane changes, which with a big motor home or trailer can be aggravating.

4. Find a specific place by first looking for it in the index. The letter–number (for example, E-5) that appears after the place will help you find it on the map. The letters correspond to those on the side margins of the map, and the numbers match those at the top and bottom. The town you want to find will be located in the area where imaginary lines drawn across the map from the "E" and the "5" intersect. If the town you are searching for is too small to be listed in the index, you can often find it on the map by looking up a bigger place you know is nearby. Not all towns on the map are listed in the index.

5. Do not depend on old maps. Most maps bear a copyright date on them. You can tell whether other maps are current by scouting out recent road construction or a rerouted highway. If the new route is not shown, your map is likely to be out of date in other ways too.

Map-wise RVers keep in mind other things about maps. North is always up. All east-west federal interstate highways carry even numbers, and all north-south federal and interstate highways carry odd numbers. Most states number their roads in this fashion, too, but not all of them. The federal highways with the lowest numbers are found in the North and East, those with the highest in the South and West. The interstate highways are the opposite, with the lowest numbers in the South and West and the highest numbers in the North and East.

To these suggestions on how to read a road map, accident-prevention experts add some final advice. They point out that it is impossible to study a map safely while whizzing along in high-speed traffic. If you are piloting yourself, the time to read your map is before you start the day's trip or at least while pulled safely off the highway. Moreover, it can add anticipation to an RV trip if you spend a few evenings at home planning your route to include interesting scenic and historical spots. Plan your itinerary so that you avoid driving through big cities during rush hours, and put your longer stints at the wheel during the middle of the week, when there are fewer cars on the road. When driving an RV, 300 to 350 miles is a reasonable distance to go in a day. This will allow for rest and lunch stops and get you into camp before dark.

Since some tunnels prohibit RVs with liquid petroleum (LP) gas systems from passing through them, you will have to avoid them. Motor clubs or the state police can give you information on such tunnels. It is also necessary to know the height of your RV so that you will know whether you can clear tunnels, bridges, underpasses, and even filling station or hotel canopies.

Jot down the route numbers of the highways you will use. Following the list and watching the maps should be the navigator's job. This leaves the driver free to concentrate on road conditions and traffic.

Preparing Your Rig

Today's rigs are comparatively trouble-free, but they need maintenance as much as do any motor vehicles. Many people avoid reading the owner's manual for the vehicle that they have bought until they are in trouble on the road. It is a good idea to read the manual for the vehicle you will be using to tow a trailer as well as the guide for the trailer. The time to read the manual for a motor home is when you are planning a trip.

If you drive a motor home, be sure to get an engine tune-up before you leave home. You will want to know that the timing on your motor is set correctly and that your ignition system is working right. Much depends upon your batteries, and you should be sure that they are strong and that the terminals are clean and the cells filled. The wheels ought to be balanced and aligned, and you should check to see that tires have the correct air pressure. It is also sensible to check your tires carefully at home to be sure that they are in good shape. While you are at it, check your spare and make certain that the gear for changing a tire is aboard your rig in an easy-to-get-at place. An inspection checklist is provided on page 86 for your ready reference before leaving on any trip. You should have two fire extinguishers aboard your RV—one in the driver's cab and the other close to the cooking area. Be sure they are in working order before you start on the trip. You should always take a well-stocked tool kit and basic RV maintenance supplies (see page 86), and *Woodall's RV Owner's Handbook* (Woodall Publishing Company, 11 N. Skokie Highway, Lake Bluff, IL 60044) is a useful repair and maintenance manual to have on hand. If you are likely to encounter subfreezing temperatures, see that your radiator is protected with antifreeze.

Equipment Checklist

Tool kit, including socket wrench, screwdrivers, and pliers
spare tire
fire extinguisher
road flares
flashlight
triangular portable reflector kit
jumper cable
spare can of oil and opener
red gasoline can
gasoline siphon hose
fan belt
fuses
roll of one-inch repair tape
owner's manual
jack
wheel blocks

Inspection Checklist

Check all fluid levels, including batteries, radiator, engine oil, power steering, brake, and transmission fluids.
If you are towing a trailer, check coupling, hitch, safety chains, and electrical and brake connections.
Connect auxiliary battery.
Tighten wheel lug nuts.
Check tire inflation.
Check running, brake, and signal lights.
Adjust mirrors.
Test trailer brakes.
Check warning bulbs and gauges.

Practicing Backing

Before you take to the road, you must be comfortable maneuvering your RV. This was on the mind of a retired executive in Park Ridge, Illinois, when he rented a trailer for his first RV trip. He considered exactly how he could back it into a campsite without making a fool of himself in front of veteran RVers, all properly backed into their spots. He went to a toy store and bought a small army truck pulling a cannon on wheels. He sat down on the living room floor and backed his truck and cannon until he had the right feel for backing a trailer. Other first-time RVers take their new trailer and its towing vehicle to the expansive parking lot of a shopping mall on a holiday when there are only a few autos present. There they practice backing their trailer until they, too, have the right feel for the operation. This certainly beats backing a trailer into a trash receptacle, the water hookup, or a tree at a campsite.

Securing Your Home

While you are enjoying a trip in your home on wheels, you will want peace of mind as to the home you leave behind you. To ward off unwelcome intruders, cancel your newspaper deliveries and make arrangements for someone to take in your mail and any circulars that may be dropped off at your home. Your house sitter can also look after your pets, plants, lawn, and garden. You should leave your itinerary so that you can be reached in case of emergency; advise the house sitter if you change your plans when you are on the trip.

If you are setting off on a long trip, you can make arrangements for such things as dividends and Social Security or other checks to be deposited automatically in your bank account. Your insurance premiums should be paid in advance so that your insurance does not expire when you are traveling. Your driver's license, your vehicle title and registration, a copy of your policy, and the name and phone number of your agent should all be in a handy place on the rig. You will probably want to carry a credit card that has cash benefits and buy traveler's checks. You can use the mail-forwarding service of an RV club (the Good Sam Club has an excellent one) to stay in touch with home base, or you can have mail forwarded to you care of General Delivery at a post office or an American Express office.

7
Packing an RV

Even the best-ordered RV sounds like a frontier Yankee peddler's wagon jingling and jangling along the highway if with every bump the flatware in the drawer rattles, a teakettle nestling in the sink clunks, and a loose chain hastily slung into an outside storage compartment clanks as if possessed. A practiced RVer is careful not to leave drawers, cabinet doors, or, above all, a refrigerator door unlatched. A sharp turn to avoid a compact that races out in front of you, and the unlatched refrigerator door flies open allowing a cascade of butter, jelly, potato salad, and whatever else the refrigerator contains to leap onto the floor.

A veteran RVer also reduces pots, pans, and dishes to basic essentials, and many replace heavier and more breakable pottery and glass dishes with plastic ones. Glass and metal containers are heavy, too, and purists even repack their jelly or honey in plastic butter tubs not only to cut down on weight but to prevent spillage. It is a good idea to make a list of household things and vehicle equipment you plan to take along and check everything as you pack it.

Some of the rattling and banging that an RV seems heir to can be prevented by a judicious use of foam rubber padding and shock cord. Fragile things that bump and thump together can get broken, so it is best to separate them with padding.

Everything in Its Proper Place

It is also reasonable to place items that are used a great deal in cabinets where they can be easily reached, and to store things that may be needed only once or twice on the trip in less accessible outside compartments. Your emergency gear—including jack, lug wrench, wheel blocks, tool kit, flares, a flashlight, and fire extinguishers—should, in particular, be easy to find should you need any of the items. Everything should be kept in its proper place in an RV because even the largest motor home or fifth-wheel travel trailer is too small to allow people to strew things around. More important than the dreary effect of clutter on the human spirit is the way things left out can become flying projectiles if the RV has to make a quick stop.

Ensuring Stability

Whether loading a motor home or a trailer, it is important to put heavy things in the lower compartments; such objects should never be strapped to the roof. Keeping the vehicle's center of gravity low will ensure that the RV is not top-heavy on the road.

When packing your rig, you should make sure to distribute the weight properly. Locate your heaviest items as close to the area over the trailer's axle as you possibly can. There are load-distributing devices that

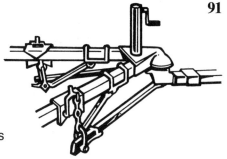

The arms of this load-equalizing hitch (recommended for trailers weighing over 2,000 pounds) help distribute the trailer's weight to all four wheels of the tow vehicle.

can be added to your hitch to help adjust the weight on the rear of your tow vehicle, but these cannot perform miracles, so you have to throttle your inclination to take along everything imaginable.

A truck camper is another matter. To ensure stability, the heaviest things should be placed forward and low. It is imperative not to put heavy objects on the rear overhang or you tend to raise your front wheels. They then have less contact to the road surface, something that in slippery weather can lead to a serious steering problem. Side-to-side balance in any RV is also important, so do not put all your heavy things on one side. Heavy items should be well secured so that they will not suddenly shift and upset the balance of your RV as you are finding your way through traffic. This creates a problem for RVers who hang a motorcycle on the rear of their camper. The motorcycle is better off on the front bumper, and its weight must be figured into your total load. When you load a motor home, locate the heaviest weight midway between the front and rear axles to give the vehicle the best balance.

An Exercise in Logistics

RVs vary considerably in the amount of storage space they offer and how it is distributed. When you are buying or renting an RV, pay close attention to the closets, cabinets, and drawers. You will invariably discover that every effort to shorten a vehicle so as to make it more convenient to drive or park in a campsite and more economical to operate also cuts out storage space. It came as an unwelcome surprise to my wife and me on a recent trip that our twenty-four-foot borrowed motor home did not have a full-length closet. This complicates the storage of clothing. John Handley, a *Chicago Tribune* reporter, took a trip in a new mini motor home from Chicago to Florida. He was amazed that so much was squeezed into so little space.

"Forget the steamer trunks and even suitcases," he noted. "You fit your clothes, food, and other gear into several small storage compartments and into the relatively spacious closet."

It becomes a real exercise in logistics to become full-timers or to take a trip lasting several months. Part of the problem is confusion over what clothing to bring. By matching what you bring to the activities and climate, you can keep clothing to a minimum. After all, why bring a business suit or perhaps an evening dress unless you know that you are going to vary your casual lifestyle with a business or social function where you have to dress up? You can keep down volume by avoiding single-use items wherever possible. Take wash-and-wear items that you can use a lot, and life will be easier. Besides, most commercial campgrounds have laundry facilities. It is not the RV style to change clothes just to make an impression. Providing you are neat and clean, you're far better off dressing casually with RVers than being fashionable.

Watching Weight

Planning your packing will help you position the items you are taking in their most appropriate places. By all means be a weight watcher. A rule of thumb used by RVers is that for every hundred pounds of weight they add to their rig, they cut down 1 percent on their fuel economy and increase wear on tires and brakes. For this reason seasoned RVers do not buy all the food they may need for an entire trip at the very start. They keep their supplies aboard the rig to a reasonable minimum unless they are going into a wilderness area where stores are few and far between. They also avoid buying heavy canned goods and take advantage of lighter weight frozen foods, providing they have a freezer aboard, or freeze-dried foods, which both keeps down weight and conserves space.

Liquids weigh a great deal. A gallon of water weighs over 8 pounds, so your rig's sixty-gallon tank may add 480 pounds to your load. You may be driving into an area where every drop aboard your RV is precious, but if you are going from one campground freshwater hookup to another, you would be well advised to make the day's drive with only as much water aboard as you need to operate the facilities and provide drinking water when on the road. Most economy-minded RVers make certain that they dump their gray water, the water from their sinks, before they take to the road if they possibly can. As for the black water, namely the sewage, it is a good idea to keep your tank at least partially full so that the chemicals that you add to its contents have some liquid on which to work.

Overloading an RV

Many RVs that you encounter as you drive down the road are overloaded beyond the safe capacity of the vehicle's suspension system. This can have a serious effect on the safe operation of the RV. When you read the owner's manual for your trailer, motor home, or truck camper, you will discover that firm load limits are recommended. RVs manufactured after January 1, 1972, also have safety certification labels attached to the hinge pillar, the door latch, or the door edge next to the driver's seat. The rig's gross vehicle weight rating (GVWR) and gross axle weight rating (GAWR) are given. You should take seriously the information in your manual dealing with the loading and weighing of the vehicles and the suggestions made as to how you should distribute the loads.

After January 1, 1973, manufacturers of truck campers were required to place a label on each rig that indicates its weight when it contains such standard equipment as freshwater tanks, bottle-gas tanks, and refrigerator—all filled to capacity. The owner's manual furnished with the camper also must provide a list of additional equipment that the camper is designed to carry along with the maximum weight for each item, providing the weight is more than twenty pounds. A statement usually required runs, "To estimate the total cargo load that will be placed on a truck, add the weight of all passengers in the camper; the weight of supplies, tools, and all other cargo; the weight of installed additional or optional camper equipment; and the manufacturer's camper weight figure."

To be sure that your truck camper is within the limits allowed, you should load it with everything that you normally take on a trip. All your fuel and water tanks should be filled, and your family should get into the truck cab. You should then drive onto a scale at a moving, coal, or trucking company or at a state weighing station along the road. First you weigh the entire vehicle to see if the total weight exceeds the truck camper's GVWR. If it does, you are going to have to leave some of your things behind. You also should weigh each axle separately to discover the weight on it. The front of the vehicle is weighed on the rear of the scale, and the rear end is weighed on the front end of the scale. If your readings exceed the weight allowed on each axle, you will have to redistribute the weight. You can also weigh each side of your rig to see to it that both sides weigh approximately the same. Motor homes should be weighed in the same way so that you do not exceed weight ratings.

You also should weigh your trailer. Pull it onto the scale, unhitch it, and weigh only the loaded trailer. Compare the weight with the weights allowed in your owner's manual specifications. You might keep in mind that a light hitch load may cause the trailer to fishtail when you drive at high speeds. On the other hand, if your hitch load is too great, you will find it hard to steer, brake, or turn your tow vehicle.

Once you have loaded your camper, motor home, or trailer properly, it is a good idea to make a note of where everything is. Many RVers make a rough diagram of their RV and note on it where they put things so that they can find them quickly when on the trip and also remember where they put them to achieve the right balance when they pack for the next trip.

On your first RV trip you are bound to take along more than you need. When you unpack the rig upon your return home, consider what things you used and what you did not use. On the next trip leave behind the things that your experience has taught you need not have been loaded aboard in the first place.

8
On the Road

A heart-of-America road can run arrow-straight across the prairie, but it can also wind among hills and forests. As a driver behind the wheel of an RV discovers, the Midwest has broad plains, but it also has the up-and-down dale country of Iowa, where covered bridges span plashy streams among green copses, and the high country of northwestern Illinois, where the old lead-mining town of Galena has hills so steep that you can look down from one street to the top of church steeples on the street below.

Discovering America

RVers can discover the United States off the interstate. They can explore such magnificent roads as the Blue Ridge Parkway through the southern Appalachians; or Route 34 in Pennsylvania from Carlisle to Gettysburg, where in the autumn the maples are brilliant; or drive through New York State's Finger Lakes region, where tart old-fashioned apples hang heavy in orchards and waterfalls splash in rocky ravines. Finger Lake roads climb the high hills and wind along the serene valleys. An RVer can take the roads built more than a century ago by Joshua Chaffee, who put them on the sunny side of the hills so that winter snows would melt away more quickly.

To the RVer on the West Coast, there are ways to escape the hurtling traffic of the freeways. Back roads skirt splendid beaches from California to Washington or corkscrew through high mountain passes. A California road heads south from Interstate 40 at Barstow to the high desert country around Twentynine Palms. After a desert rain the flowers burst into bloom, a testimony to the fertility of the land when the magic of water is brought to it. Some states publish booklets that suggest scenic ways to avoid the monotony of the interstates. Tennessee's parkway system, for example, covers 2,300 miles of highways that tie together the state's parks, major lakes, historical sites, and recreational attractions. The Department of Tourism has put up two thousand highway signs along these roads; each is surmounted by the mockingbird, the Tennessee state bird, so that motorists can "follow the mockingbird" to get the most enjoyment out of a trip through the state.

Enjoying People

To an RVer on the road, it is not just the highway and the landscape but the people who give savor to a journey. Between Washington and Baltimore is tranquil countryside. It is a great place to roam the open roads, letting one charming back road lead to another, one experience flow naturally into another.

In Frederick, Maryland, a woman sat on her front porch, her tiny grandson on her lap. Ranked about her on the porch and its rails were fanciful carved animals and toys. There was no sign to indicate anything was for sale, but when we stopped to talk to her, she said shyly, "Yes, I'll sell any of the critters." Her husband carved the figures, and she painted them. They were authentic folk art, and the prices she asked ranged from two to six dollars. Anyone who stopped by found not only a bargain but a chance to talk with a woman who expressed in her smiles and every word an inner serenity, which proved marvelously catching.

There is a surprising peace of mind in RV touring because whenever you want to make a rest stop, eat a snack, or simply sip a soft drink, you can always pull into a roadside park or some other spot where you are well off the pavement and find everything at your fingertips. It is striking how seeing the passing scene from the high driver's cab of an RV or from a motor home's broad windows turns out to be so much more intimate an experience than seeing the same sights from a nearer-to-the-pavement auto. Being up high gives an RVer a big picture, a better perspective on things.

A Safe Way to Go

Travel in an RV is also a safe way to go, but there are certain demands put upon an RV driver that the driver of an auto does not have to consider. These demands begin even before an RVer pulls out of a campsite. The checklist on page 113 will guide an RVer in preparing to leave a campsite. It is especially important that once the vehicle is disconnected from the campground's hookups, the pilot light on any appliance be turned off, and the valves of the liquid petroleum tanks be closed. Having a pilot flame on in the rig when it is near a gasoline station fuel pump is a dangerous thing.

Most RVers like to start off on a drive early in the day, when the traffic is less, and when, in the summertime, it is cooler. And some, whose eyes are bothered by the sun, recommend timing your travel so that you are never driving into the rising or setting sun. Others say this is nonsense and the time to go is when you feel like it. Many retired people in particular believe that there will be plenty of time to start off down the road after they have had a leisurely breakfast and a chance to say farewell in a relaxed way to their campground neighbors. At least everybody agrees that it is a very good idea to avoid city traffic during rush hours and to get out of a city and onto the open road by the most direct route. Stop-and-go city driving is exasperating and wastes gasoline.

Once on the road an experienced RV driver saves gasoline in other ways too. For each five miles per hour over fifty miles per hour, the mileage drops one mile per gallon. An RVer understands better than most motorists how the speed limit of fifty-five miles per hour does truly conserve fuel. Equally important, RVers know they should not jackrabbit. A fast getaway, an abrupt stop, sporadic bursts of speed, and continual lane changes for fleeting advantages in traffic are not only hard on passengers and gear within the vehicle but also costly in fuel economy. On an interstate in an RV, reach cruising speed and stick to it as much as possible. If there is cruise control, set it and then just relax. When a stoplight appears in the distance, glide down from cruising speed to a stop with a minimum expenditure of braking energy. Speed up at the sight of a steep hill ahead to make the climb with the least strain on the engine. On a downgrade, gear down if it is truly steep and let the motor act as a brake. This prevents brake fade, particularly if the driver pumps the brakes to help keep them cool.

"Many motor homes are big, high, and wide," cautions the National Highway Traffic Safety Administration. "The added height and configuration of a . . . camper make it more susceptible to tip-over in a sudden turning movement. With both motor homes and . . . campers you have a great deal of weight that must be controlled. All these characteristics make it necessary for the operators of such vehicles to become thoroughly familiar with their handling characteristics and to take special precautions while driving on the highway, especially when making turns, changing lanes, passing, and controlling speed on downgrades."

A vehicle towing a trailer requires even more careful handling. All recreation vehicles take longer to stop or to accelerate, have a different turning radius and a higher center of gravity, and need more overhead and side clearance than do cars.

An RV simply cannot accelerate as fast as an auto. This means that you must allow more space when you merge onto an expressway, drive onto a busy highway from a side road or from a stop by the road, or make a left turn at an intersection. Passing other vehicles also takes extra space, and plenty of it at that. If you err in your judgment and have to cut in sharply to avoid oncoming traffic, you run the grave risk of a skid, oversteering, sway, or if you are pulling a trailer, fish-tailing, which can throw a tow vehicle right off the road. One trick that veteran RVers know is to keep an eye on the exhaust of the vehicle that you are starting to pass on a two-lane road. As the National Safety Council puts it, "A puff of smoke tells you that the driver is speeding up, alerting you to take whatever defensive measures are necessary to avoid a crash." It is essentially true that the bigger the RV, the more care should be exerted in driving it.

Because of their bulk and weight, RVs cannot stop suddenly. RVers are urged to allow one second for every ten feet of vehicle length, but never less than four seconds.

"Begin to count as the vehicle passes some fixed point on the roadside, such as a tree or signpost," suggests the Commonwealth of Virginia Division of Motor Vehicles. "This formula is good for all rigs at all speeds, and maintaining a safe 'space cushion' is the single most important driving technique you can develop."

An RVer should add several seconds if the road is wet and slippery with rain and even more seconds if it is icy. Some RVers ensure that they have enough space between their rig and the vehicle ahead of them by using a simple formula. For every ten miles per hour they are moving, they maintain a distance of at least one length of their motor home or the combined length of their tow vehicle and trailer. For a 30-foot vehicle traveling at fifty miles per hour, this means following the vehicle ahead by 150 feet.

While you are preserving your space cushion around your rig by staying well behind the vehicle ahead of you, you also are giving yourself the opportunity to see farther ahead on the road. Following too close to a truck or another RV that blocks out what is ahead is patently dangerous, since an RVer needs to see farther down the road than does a driver of a smaller vehicle, which can stop more quickly or dodge around such things as a break in the pavement or debris that may have fallen from a truck. Just as a jumbo-sized vehicle ahead of you may block your view of the road, your RV most likely will block the view of a driver behind you. When you see a stop is likely, you should slow as gradually as is safe and avoid jamming on the brakes in a panic stop. If you have time, you should first flash your brake lights a couple of times to let the motorists behind you know that you are preparing to make a stop.

A smaller vehicle may be able to swerve around an obstacle in the road, but such a zigzag can throw an RV out of control. Your safety depends on making a straight-line stop as smoothly as you possibly can. With your heavy rig you should avoid locking your brakes, since locked wheels skid and cut down on your stopping power.

Turning Your Rig

A large rig, with its wheel base longer than that of a car, requires that you cut much wider when you turn, or you are likely to bump your rear wheel against the curb. It will come naturally with practice, but at first it seems odd that you must move farther into the intersection before starting to turn. If you are pulling a trailer, you turn from the center of the intersection into the right side of the lane and then bring your tow vehicle and the trailer into the center of it. Most RVers use the hand-over-hand steering motion so that they have their rig under tight control throughout the entire maneuver.

Even a curve on a highway needs to be negotiated with care. The suggested safe turning speeds posted on many U.S. roads are intended for automobiles. Your RV, with its high center of gravity, will sway if you try to take a turn too fast, and you should be more conservative than an auto driver need be when it comes to speeds with which you take the curve. If you curve to the right, stay to the center of your lane so that the rear wheels will not leave the pavement. If you curve to the left, stay more to the right of your lane so that the back of your rig will not cross over into the lane intended for oncoming traffic.

Watching for Overhead Obstructions

One of the common errors of a driver at the wheel of a rented or newly purchased RV is to bump its roof into the overhang of a filling station, shopping mall, or motel. Tree branches shading an idyllic side road may hang low enough to thump on the roof, and there are a few underpasses low enough to prevent passage. It is important to know from the start what the vehicle's clearance is and to keep a keen eye on the signs that adorn most overhangs and underpasses advising motorists as to how many feet and inches they will allow. All of this becomes second nature to RV drivers, and they learn to tell at a glance whether their vehicle will fit. They also learn never to take a chance, and if there is a questionable branch or any other overhead hazard, they have a companion get out and walk them through as they creep ahead beneath the obstacle.

Ground Clearances

RVs usually have a higher ground clearance than autos, but it is a good idea to inspect the underside of your vehicle so that you know exactly what you have to deal with. If your RV does drag on a mucky country road or in a parking lot where you are attempting to turn around, you have a lot more to extricate. You want to avoid bumps and holes that might break a spring or an axle. If you have any doubt about the road surface, have somebody walk ahead of you to be sure it is safe. When you come out of some driveways or pass through a dip on the road (a common occurrence in the desert Southwest), your tow vehicle will be coming up while the trailer is still going down. This causes the hitch to be thrust toward the pavement, which can create a rude scraping sound, and you can get stuck in that position. While visiting a ghost town in New Mexico, I once snagged our hitch in a desert arroyo. There was nothing to do but unfasten it with considerable labor. At least the experience was as educational as it was irritating.

Buffeting Winds

Buffeting winds can also be a problem for an RV. Driving in a motor home across New Mexico on Interstate 10, a desert sandstorm swirled about and darkened the sky. Tumbleweed scurried across the road. When a wind devil danced toward the rig, I held tight to the wheel because I realized how it could wrench an RV. The devil shrieked and flung sagebrush and pebbles around the rig. It shook the vehicle and for an instant seemed to lift it from the highway. I wished that I had slowed the vehicle more than I had because perhaps then the wind devil might have passed ahead, or at least my wheels would have had a better grip on the pavement and the RV would not have careened so badly. An RV may be heavy, but its sides are long and flat and not exactly aerodynamic.

My wife and I had scarcely driven much farther into Arizona when we picked up repeated announcements on our radio from the Arizona State Police advising motor homes and vehicles pulling trailers to stay out of the region of high winds, which stretched across the center part of that state. When we reached the area, we discovered that the wind warnings had been lifted, and the desert was quiet.

At a roadside stop on I-10 between Tucson and Phoenix on a recent RV trip, I read a posted warning that explained to out-of-state drivers that dust storms strike quickly in Arizona, particularly on I-10 between Phoenix and Tucson and on I-5 from Gila Bend to Casa Grande. They can precipitate chain accidents. The warning advised that in a dust storm, drivers should pull as far off the highway as possible, stop, turn the vehicle's lights off, set the emergency brake, and be sure that the brake lights are off. Other drivers trying to maneuver under these low-visibility conditions may be confused by brake lights, which they will assume indicate the direction of the road. The warning also advised motorists who could not get off the pavement to drive at a reduced speed, turn the lights on, and use the center line as a guide. No matter what else, a vehicle should never stop on the pavement. Such dust-storm warnings are of equal value to a driver at the wheel of an auto or an RV, and a CB radio can be of particular value in regions of turbulent weather.

Buffeting winds, which are encountered almost anywhere on the road, seem to be particularly dangerous to RVs in the deserts of the Southwest. In the deserts around Palm Springs, California, wind socks are flown from time to time along the roads so that RVers can judge the direction and strength of the wind. When there are wind alerts, it is sensible for an RVer to shelter in a campground, roadside park, service station, or some other secure spot until the winds die down.

Encountering Trucks and Buses

A semitrailer truck or bus can be a problem too. If you meet one on the road, it may cause considerable turbulence around your rig, but the most serious wind currents swirl around you when the vehicle passes from behind. The air rushing over the front of the cab will push you to the side of the road, only to have the currents whipped up by the rear of the vehicle drag you violently back. This push and drag sways your RV so that, if you are not prepared for it, you may be forced off the road. This can be particularly dangerous if you are pulling a trailer, since, while the tow vehicle is getting the full pushing effect of the wind from the truck's cab, the trailer may be already getting the opposite pulling effect of the wind from the truck's rear. This can set up a wild fishtailing that is hard to bring under control.

David Tarrant, Ford's RV expert, adds, "If you are about to be passed while towing a trailer, try to hold a straight course. Extreme changes in steering can cause your trailer to fishtail, sometimes so severely you might lose control."

There is no way to eliminate entirely the buffeting effect of a passing truck or bus, but you can cut it down to manageable proportions by observing some precautions. As you drive down the highway in your motor home, keep checking in your rearview mirrors for the approach of a big vehicle. If you see one swing out to pass you, take your foot off the gas and move as far to the right as the pavement will allow you to go. You want to slow your rig by five to ten miles per hour to enable the passing vehicle to get by in less time and thus decrease air turbulence. If you slow too much, you will lose this effect. It is a different matter if you are pulling a trailer.

"To minimize trailer sway caused by the air displaced by a passing vehicle," suggests David Tarrant, "you should accelerate slightly." Then you should edge over in your lane as far as you safely can to increase the space between your rig and the passing vehicle. It is imperative not to be coasting when the truck or bus passes you, or the trailer is likely to start swaying. If you are going downhill when the vehicle passes you, you can get the same control over the trailer by gently applying the trailer brakes alone, since the idea in all cases is to increase the tension on the hitch.

If the driver passing you is a good one, he or she will observe what you are doing and will in turn move as far to the left as possible. This will put the largest amount of space between the two vehicles and cut down on the buffeting.

A number of other conditions can cause a trailer to fishtail or sway. Crosswinds, slippery pavements, a sharp turn, or too light a hitch weight are all possibilities. Before you take to the road, you should have an effective antisway device installed by your dealer to cut down on this problem. Also, you should remember not to panic if sway or fishtailing does occur. If your trailer starts acting up, accelerate smoothly and apply the trailer brakes alone. This will bring the trailer back under control. Above all, do not jam on your brakes.

Backing an RV

Backing an RV safely is also something worth your consideration. Most drivers ask someone to go to the rear of the rig to watch through the window or, better still, have somebody outside the rig on the driver's side give instructions. Be sure to prearrange signals and words with clear-cut meanings, particularly when you are backing into a campground, since one of the common sources of entertainment among veteran RVers is to sip a cooling drink at their own picnic bench while observing the confused directions between an inexperienced observer and a driver. A number of compact

TV installations are now available to keep a driver apprised of what is behind the rig. The screen is mounted where the driver can easily see it. An ultrawide lens is mounted on the rear of the vehicle so that the driver can see such things as a small car that may have pulled behind the vehicle or a child on a bike who has stopped in what would be a blind spot without the TV monitor.

Backing a motor home is easy once you get the hang of it; backing a trailer, however, is trickier. A trailer jackknifes with appalling ease. If it does jackknife, all you can do is pull ahead and start over. The Commonwealth of Virginia Division of Motor Vehicles manual on RV safety explains the correct procedure succinctly: "With the trailer and tow vehicle in a straight line and the tow vehicle wheels straight, place your hand at the bottom of the steering wheel. If you want the rear of a trailer to go to the right, move your hand to the right. If you want the back of the trailer to go to the left, move your hand to the left. This method eliminates having to remember that a trailer reacts opposite to the way the tow vehicle wheels are turned. Once you get the trailer going in the direction you want it to go, slowly turn the steering wheel so that the tow vehicle is 'following' the trailer. From then on make small adjustments of the steering wheel to keep the trailer moving in the right direction. Backing must be done slowly and with small movements of the steering wheel; oversteering will make the trailer jackknife almost instantly."

Taking Frequent Stops

Frequent stops to enjoy the attractions along the road—everything from museums to parks, historic sites, and, perhaps, a factory to be toured—not only

make the trip more pleasurable but also make it safer.
Wise RVers know that it is not how far they drive in a
day that makes a trip worthwhile but the variety and
interest of the experiences per mile that really matter.
RVers also stop to walk about for good health's sake.

Getting off the Road Early

Most RVers prefer to get off the road by late afternoon
so that they can get a good campsite and relax before
dinner. It is also a good idea to avoid driving at night,
which is prime accident time. Dr. Herschel W. Leibowitz, professor of psychology and a leading expert on
visual perception at Pennsylvania State University, explains that your chances of being killed in a nighttime
accident are three to four times greater than in a day-
time accident. Our ability to orient ourselves is automatic, explains the professor, but our ability to
recognize is extremely dependent upon the amount of
light available. During the day, both abilities operate
at their peak. At night, our automatic orientation system continues to operate without our conscious aware-
ness. This gives us a sense of confidence in our driving
ability that is not supported by our recognition system,
which is impaired at night. Dr. Leibowitz believes that
improved headlights and reduced speeds would help at
night, but nothing helps like getting off the road before
dusk, especially when you are in unknown territory
and driving a big rig.

Emergencies on the Road

Breakdowns on the road were regular features of a
day's drive during the time of the Tin Can Tourists. Al-

though such breakdowns are infrequent today, they do happen. The most common problem is a flat tire. The National Safety Council (NSC) advises that "a good grip on the wheel helps control the vehicle, and gradual braking is imperative. Get your rig off the highway into a position that is not a hazard. Interstate shoulders are wide enough, but on secondary roads caution should be used when pulling onto a shoulder. It may or may not be able to handle the weight."

The NSC further advises that you get all occupants out of the RV and stand clear.

"Put out flares, flags, or reflective triangles—one ten to fifteen feet behind the vehicle and another 100 feet behind. If you can't get completely off the trafficway, place another 300 feet to the rear. On two-lane roads, place another warning 100 feet in front," concludes the NSC. If you do not have flashers on your disabled vehicle, raise the hood and tie a white cloth to your antenna or roadside handle.

If the rig is parked on a grade, the RVer is well advised to put the transmission in park and set the parking brake before placing wedges against the wheels. It may be sufficient to put a jack under the bumper of a car, but it must be put under the frame of either a trailer or motor home.

The second most common problem for RVs on the road is overheating. This is particularly true in the desert, at high altitudes, or on hot summer days when you have failed to brush off the hapless butterflies and insects that encrust your radiator. If you notice that your motor is beginning to get hot and your air conditioner is operating, turn the latter off. If the temperature continues to climb, pull off the road, set the parking brake, and put the transmission in park. You should open the hood, but do not touch the radiator cap. The engine should be put at a fast idle to increase the air flow. Most RVers take along an extra fan belt, since a broken fan belt is a likely cause for overheating, and carry a well-equipped tool kit to make repairs on the spot.

Some dealers or manufacturers have 800 numbers you can call to find out the nearest trustworthy repair place. Many RV clubs have a similar service. The Good Sam Club has a national network of members—who keep in mind the Good Samaritan tradition, which gave the club its name in the first place. They can usually come to your disabled rig to make minor repairs or suggest garages where you can have things put right at a fair price.

The National Institute for Automotive Service Excellence (ASE) suggests that when you have to have repairs made on a trip, you look for ASE's blue-and-white sign on the garage or service station. This means that the establishment employs at least one mechanic who is ASE certified. Certified mechanics may wear a blue-and-white shoulder patch and carry a card listing their areas of certification. Employers also may display their certified mechanic's credentials.

Ask to see the mechanic's credentials in order to determine whether the employee is qualified to make the repairs you need on your vehicle. ASE certifies mechanics in eight categories, such as brakes and engine performance. A mechanic who is an expert on brakes may not necessarily be an expert on transmissions.

Courtesy Counts

RV drivers over the years have earned something of a truck driver's reputation for courtesy and helpfulness to motorists in trouble. Veteran RVers know that courtesy is the very essence of safety and that driving a motor home or pulling a trailer leaves no room for either the hurry habit that afflicts so many motorists or for irritation at the delays and frustrations that occur in all driving. Too much depends on keeping a cool head when you are driving an RV. If you see an RVer hogging the highway, refusing to pull over to the side and let a string of cars get by, you can be sure you are looking at a rookie, a person who still has not captured either any sense of how to drive safely or the very spirit of the RV lifestyle.

Departure Checklist

Disconnect and store electrical, water, and sewer lines.
Close holding-tank valve.
Secure LP-gas bottles and turn off gas.
Turn off LP-gas appliances.
Clear counters and tables.
Close and latch cabinets and closets.
Secure refrigerator door and storage compartments.
Close and secure vents and windows.
Turn off interior lights.
Turn off water pump.
Turn off separate twelve-volt system.
Put window shield, awning, and antenna down.
Lock door and retract step.
Make last-minute check around RV to be sure everything is on board, stored, and secured.

9
Choosing a Campground

My wife and I sipped our cooling drinks beside the swimming pool and listened to a pair of cowboy singers harmonize. Their songs were punctuated by the thunk of tennis balls from the courts beyond the pool. As the shadows from the San Jacinto Mountains lengthened, we sniffed the aroma of steaks broiling and finally trooped into the clubhouse to a buffet dinner that would do justice to a plush resort. If it were not for the ranks of recreation vehicles, each tucked behind its own emerald-green lawn and shaded by palms, we might have been at such a resort. In fact, we were at a camp resort operated by the Outdoor Resorts of America in the desert outside Palm Springs, California.

We were on a two-week RV trip throughout the southwestern desert to sample a broad range of campgrounds. We were going to end up camped with one other RV in a Navajo-operated campground with a gale-force wind pummeling our rig, but tonight we were in the lap of luxury. If we desired, we not only

115

A Resort Campground in Palm Springs, California

had tennis courts, swimming pools, and bathhouses at our disposal but also heated whirlpools, a complete health club and sauna, gymnasium, a billiard room, an eighteen-hole golf course, and a gourmet restaurant awaiting our pleasure. Camp resorts such as this one are proliferating throughout the United States, and they represent one luxurious extreme of contemporary RV travel.

KOA Has Come a Long Way

A few nights later we parked our rig at the new Kampgrounds of America (KOA) Phoenix West. Once again there was a swimming pool and a clubhouse, and that evening a bunch of us roughed it by spearing steaks on three-pronged pitchforks and broiling them over a bed of aromatic mesquite coals. We helped ourselves to a Western buffet and sat down around a campfire to listen to a young cowboy strum his guitar and sing range ballads. Kampgrounds of America has come a long way since the first campground with that name was hewn out of the forest on the banks of the Yellowstone at Billings, Montana, in 1962.

By the following night we had meandered as far south as the desert west of Tucson, where we again lived in luxury at the Western Way Resort. In case we became bored with the swimming pool, the therapy pool, the card and game rooms, the library, the shuffleboard courts, and other such amenities, we could cross the road into Tucson Mountain Park and hike a trail to see a variety of birds and other wildlife in a protected preserve. Because childish trebles or adolescent hootings might distract from the adult calm of the place, children are excluded from the campgrounds from October through April.

Camping in the Woods

Children were certainly welcome at the next night's camp, for we drove to the Coconino National Forest, north of Flagstaff, and parked our RV in Bonito Campground. Ponderosa pine towered over our campsite and dropped their needles on our picnic bench. Other RVers who had driven into the camp early had started warming fires against the high country chill in the fireplaces at their sites, and we bantered and told stories while the sun dropped behind the looming San Francisco Mountains. A coyote yipped, and when the dark came, it was total. There were no well-tended lawns, no at-the-rig garbage service, no night-lights, no water, no electricity, and no sewage connections, but there were spotlessly clean washrooms with indoor plumbing. In the dusk two boys tossed a baseball back and forth, and later a baby cried at the far end of the campground. Across the road was a magnificent view of the snowcapped San Francisco Mountains, the highest peaks in Arizona, and a vast national forest reached all around us. Within half an hour of our awakening the next morning, we were hiking a trail through the lava beds of the adjacent Wupatki National Monument.

The following night our RV was snuggled up to the full hookups of the Trailer Village within strolling distance of Yavapai Lodge on the south rim of the Grand Canyon National Park. Once again we had spic-and-span washrooms provided by the national park campground concessionaire just in case we found it inconvenient to use the facilities aboard our rig.

We lingered a few days because there are so many fascinating things to do at the Grand Canyon, but then we drove off to Monument Valley to continue our campground research. There we stayed at another KOA just across the border in Gouldings, Utah. Red rock cliffs rose beside the campground, and a Navajo girl dropped by to talk. The next morning an Indian at the wheel of his off-road vehicle picked us up at the campground and took us deep into the valley to remote beauty spots. A twelve-year-old Indian lad trotted up on his horse and obligingly struck a pose on a rocky point overlooking the vast sweep of the desert studded with towering rock formations. We were forced back to our rig by a sandstorm that stung our faces and made breathing difficult.

Camping with Indians

We stayed on at the KOA campground another night and then drove a few miles away to Two Mittens Campground, operated by the Navajos atop a bluff over-looking the valley. There we watched a violent thunder-and-lightning storm careen out of the west. The wind shook our rig. The Indians did not provide any hookups, but their fee was nominal and the wash-rooms clean, even if coins were required to turn on the showers. Young Navajos came around to tidy up the camp and to talk about their people and their own fu-tures, and a party of teenage West German boys and girls, all members of a German future farmers move-ment, set up their tents. Half the fun of camping is meeting other people, and the German youngsters, ex-cited by the vast sweep of the American West, were good companions. One boy almost stepped on a snake that rattled ominously to warn him off.

"Just think," he chortled to a friend, "wait until I get home and tell my girlfriend that I almost got bit by an American rattlesnake!"

In the morning we drove off to Canyon de Chelly Monument, where we set up our rig in the camp-ground a few hundred yards from the visitors' center at the mouth of the canyon. The campground was free, and there were clean rest rooms, but no hookups. There was a dumping station, which we used before we took to the road. Once again we enlisted an Indian and his four-wheel drive to ride deep into the canyon to in-spect the intriguing prehistoric cliff dwellings. No RV or conventional auto is allowed in the canyon, which is just as well, since we had hardly been on the canyon floor for ten minutes when we happened upon two Na-vajo pickups, both stuck in quicksand.

Our next destination was the Petrified Forest Na-tional Park, where there is no campground. We ar-rived at the small town nearest the park entrance and thought of boondocking at a truck stop, but we con-cluded that the sound of trucks snorting past on the adjacent interstate would not be conducive to slumber. We drove on some forty miles to Holbrook, where we stayed at a commercial campground, far enough from the interstate for peace. There were full hookups, a Laundromat, and a camp store, where we could replenish supplies.

"Members Only" Camping

Our last campground of the trip was a Thousand Trails location in Verde Valley, north of Phoenix. We had been offered a free night's camping to get acquainted with this members-only camp resort, and the guard at the gate let us in without hassle. We hooked up our rig next to the Verde River. Other campers met us as if we were boon companions, but we were too late for the movie in the clubhouse and too tired from hiking around the petrified forest to take advantage of the swimming pool or the opportunity to angle for catfish and bass in the stream. At least we had the chance to sample still another type of campground that has become popular across the land.

Camping in Back Country

On RV trips over the years, we have stayed at the fanciest of camp resorts and boondocked in school yards in Montana villages or out on the range beside the California Trail. We have never felt threatened or in any way uneasy about camping alone, though it did give us a start to be aroused from sleep one night in northeastern Utah by something heavy bumping against our rig. We peered out the window to discover that a herd of several hundred range cattle had clustered around us for the night, and one was scratching its itchy bovine head against the corner of our vehicle. Once, we drew up our truck camper next to the sleeping wagon of a Basque sheepherder on a remote stretch of the Oregon Trail in the Idaho panhandle. He was trembling with a mixture of outrage and terror because only a few hours before, a party of cattlemen had ridden their horses through his camp, upsetting his cooking pot where it simmered over the fire and slashing the canvas of his wagon. He was glad to see us and begged us to stay with him overnight.

"They'll never come back with you folks camping here," he said.

We stayed on without the slightest fear but with a strong sense of sharing in the reality of the West, where cattlemen and sheepherders still do not get along on ranges far removed from the interstates and passing state patrol cars.

Campground for the Night

All RVers have their own feelings about the kinds of campgrounds they prefer, and we have ours. As a rule, we use commercial campgrounds, both those franchised or owned by the big national chains and those owned by the people who run them, when we are traveling across the country and simply need a comfortable and convenient place for the night. Some of these campgrounds are seedy, but most that are listed in the major campground directories are clean and appealing. People in them are generally friendly, and they almost always have hookups and other services that an RVer may need. They also are often so close to the interstates or some other important highway that passing trucks seem about to run right through your rig. On several occasions we have belatedly discovered that the highway is on one side of the campground and a railroad on the other, and that the railroad, through no matter how rural a countryside, is surprisingly busy at night. Most commercial campgrounds offer sites only big enough for a rig, a picnic table, and possibly a grill, and the RVs are packed cheek by jowl in the sort of unwelcome comradery that sardines experience in a can. Still, some of our happiest experiences have been in privately owned camps, and they are an integral part of RV travel.

Some RVers spend more money than necessary on commercial camps. If you are just stopping for the night and have no intention of using the swimming pool, miniature golf course, or shuffleboard court, there is no point in paying a premium rate to stay at a campground with those facilities. Just down the road there may be another camp, which doesn't have a pool or other entertainment but charges a third to a half less. The most expensive campground we have ever stayed at is Fort Wilderness at Disney World in Florida, and the Disney people say right out that it is probably the most expensive campground in the world. They also are quick to point out that there is free transportation from the campground to both Disney World and Epcot Center and that, compared with staying in a hotel close to the attractions, it is relatively inexpensive. Then, too, where else can you go to a campfire presided over by such characters as Mickey Mouse and Chip 'n Dale? All of this is good fun, but it makes the point with appropriate emphasis: there is no sense in paying a premium rate just to spend the night in a campground, but if the facilities themselves have attracted you and you plan to use them, the more expensive campgrounds are well worth the extra charge.

Membership and Shared-Time Resorts

Controversial among RVers are membership and shared-time resorts, but they, too, offer good value to people who use them often and enjoy living in a resort atmosphere with a variety of facilities and planned activities. At the latest count made by the Go Camping America Committee, there were 450 camp resorts located throughout the United States, including both the membership and the ownership varieties. They do not represent value if all you are looking for is a place to park your rig for the night or merely plan to use the campground as a base to explore the surrounding countryside.

Public Campgrounds

Some RVers prefer public parks for a transient stay, simply because they are cheaper. Their sites may not be as level, their washrooms may not be as well kept, and often there are no hookups, but they are usually more spacious and shaded by trees. A night in a woods seems more restful to most RVers when compared with a night in a packed private campground too close to traffic.

National parks and monuments, national forests, the Bureau of Land Management, the Tennessee Valley Authority, the Corps of Engineers, national wildlife refuges, state parks and forests, and some county and municipal parks offer RV camping opportunities. There are some camping surprises for those who look for them. The Wisconsin State Fair, for one, provides an RV park less than ten minutes from downtown Milwaukee. During the 1985 season the campground hosted 5,709 campers, with as many as 200 there on one night when the fair was in progress. There is also the Shoreline RV Park in the heart of downtown Long Beach, California, within sight of the ocean liner *Queen Mary* and the huge geodesic dome that covers Howard Hughes's plane, the *Spruce Goose,* which has a wingspan longer than a football field.

Scout Campgrounds

The Boy Scouts invite adult scouting volunteers and their families to bring their rigs to many of the Scout reservations and camps throughout the nation. Most Scout camps offer camping opportunities to registered volunteers from anywhere in the country, and not just those who are members of a local council. Some have space available at any time of the year, but others do not accept campers when their facilities are already fully occupied by the Scouts themselves. Local councils can advise campers on their policy. The armed forces also operate several recreation areas with RV facilities for military personnel and their families. One of the newest is the DeGray Lake Military Recreational Area near Bismarck, Arkansas. Typically, at DeGray Lake eight of the seventeen sites are reserved for servicemen on active duty and their families, but others may be used by members of the National Guard or Reserves, retired military personnel, and Defense Department civilians and their families.

Indian Campgrounds

Several American Indian tribes have established campgrounds, which offer facilities ranging from primitive to resortlike. Some utility companies have created camping and recreation areas around their reservoirs and have opened the grounds to the public. There are even one-time strip mines that have been restored to attractive natural environmental areas with camping facilities as part of the picture. The Appalachian Power Company has opened campgrounds at Smith Mountain Lake in the Cherokee Highlands of South Carolina, and the Philadelphia Electric Company welcomes RVers to Muddy Run Recreation Park at their power reservoir in the heart of Lancaster County's Pennsylvania Dutch country.

Differences in Federal Campgrounds

The various camping possibilities offer different kinds of experiences. Most of the campgrounds under the jurisdiction of the National Park Service are operated by concessionaires, and they exist in the main for the convenience of people seeking to enjoy the scenic, historic, and natural attractions of the parks and monuments. National Forest Service camps are usually more primitive and rarely have hookups; RVers who camp in these must have self-contained units. The camps provide more space and are close to such things as hiking and backpacking trails, canoeing and fishing streams, crags to be climbed, and wildlife and geological formations to be studied. Bureau of Land Management camping areas are even more primitive when it comes to facilities and usually offer only a few sites in a remote spot. Tennessee Valley Authority and Corps of Engineer sites are likely to be close to aquatic activities, such as swimming, boating, and wind surfing. Fishing goes hand in hand with boating when it comes to the activities enjoyed by RVers who prefer these sites. As might be expected, state parks and forests tend to follow the patterns set by national parks and forests, but state forests have additional appeal in that they are far less known; there are often campsites going begging in a state forest close to a national park that is jammed with RVs. At least there is something to appeal to just about all the 25 million people who every year go camping in travel trailers, motor homes, folding camping trailers, and other types of RVs.

The National Forest Service administers 154 forests covering 200 million acres of land, with 100,000 miles of trails, 70,000 miles of streams and rivers, and some 7,000 developed campgrounds. If you want to camp in a national forest, you can obtain a free list of all the forests and their addresses by writing to the Forest Service, U.S. Department of Agriculture, Office of Information, PO Box 2417, Washington, DC 20013.

There are four hundred national park areas ranging from such world-famous beauty spots as the Grand Canyon and Yellowstone to lesser known places such as Cumberland Gap. As a rule the lesser known places attract fewer campers. The Great Smokey Mountains National Park is the most popular of all the national parks, and the park and all the nearby private campgrounds are usually jam-packed during the summer months; yet Cumberland Gap, to the north between Virginia and Kentucky, will have spaces open and fascinating things to enjoy—including a mountain trail that leads to pioneer villages and the actual Wilderness Trail, over which Daniel Boone traveled into Kentucky. *Camping in the National Park System* can be ordered for $1.50 from the U.S. Government Printing Office, Superintendent of Documents, Washington, DC 20402.

The National Wildlife Refuge System is managed by the U.S. Fish and Wildlife Service and includes 428 refuge systems located in forty-nine states, often beneath flightways used by migrating fowl. Campers who appreciate birds and wildlife particularly value the chance to stay in one of the refuges. Only some of the refuges offer camping to RVs. If you want a list of those that do, write to the U.S. Fish and Wildlife Service, Public Affairs Office, Washington, DC 20240.

The Bureau of Land Management oversees 280 million acres of outdoor recreation lands in the western states and in Alaska. For information on the camping areas open to RVs, write the Bureau of Land Management, Public Affairs Office, 1800 C Street, NW, Washington, DC 20240.

There are 53,000 campsites in the U.S. Army Corps of Engineers areas. They are almost all near lakes, rivers, and oceans. To obtain a free list of district offices, where you can obtain camping information about the region in which you live or plan to visit, send your request and a stamped, self-addressed envelope to U.S. Army Corps of Engineers, 20 Massachusetts Avenue, NW, Washington, DC 20314; mark it to the attention of the Public Affairs Office. The locations of camps in state parks and forests and county and municipal parks are listed in the leading campground directories available in bookstores and libraries, and state tourism authorities can usually send you information on them. Some states publish directories of both the public and private campgrounds within their borders.

The Indians offer some of the most fascinating of camping opportunities.

"Hon dah," say the Apaches to families who visit the Fort Apache Reservation in Arizona. This translates as "Be my guest."

Families who bring their children to visit the Apaches in their forested mountains northeast of

Phoenix learn that the Indians will show them how to hunt and fish the Indian way. Families vacationing among the Apaches discover that their reservation has three hundred miles of well-stocked trout streams and the largest forests of ponderosa in the nation, high country lakes, big game, and fascinating places left from the Indian wars. They find that the Apaches welcome visitors with unmistakable friendliness. They even pile up firewood at the campsites.

When the redoubtable Apaches decided to welcome campers, other tribes followed, and today you can visit the Indians from Florida to Alaska. The Navajos offer camping at tribal parks not only at Monument Valley but also at Lake Powell and Little Colorado River Gorge. The Utes of Utah invite visitors to Bottle Hollow Reservoir. Farther north in Montana, the Crows offer fine camping in the Big Horn Canyon Recreation Area and put on a dramatic outdoor reenactment of the Custer Battle at Crow Agency. The Blackfeet possess one of the most scenic reservations of all. It adjoins Glacier National Park, and there are campsites at Chewing Backbone, Duck Lake, and Two Medicine. Indian tribes that live along the Washington coast also provide camping facilities and advise RVers, "You don't have to make a reservation to camp on a reservation." Nor are all the Indian campgrounds in the West. The Seneca nation invites campers to use its Highbanks Campground on the Allegheny Indian Reservation situated on the Allegheny Reservoir in northwestern Pennsylvania.

Reserving a Campsite

Whether you camp courtesy of the Indians, the forest service, or state parks, you are well advised to get to your campsite early. Some campgrounds accept reservations, and others do not; some allow the public to reserve certain sites while offering other sites on a first-come/first-served basis. A nationwide computer reservation system reserves campsites for some national parks and state parks. You can make reservations at some campgrounds throughout the country by writing to Ticketron, PO Box 2715, San Francisco, CA 94126, or by going to a Ticketron box office in a department store or a shopping mall near your home. Some states also offer computerized reservation services for campgrounds at tourist information and welcome centers located at their borders on principal highways. Alabama pioneered this service, but Tennessee and Kentucky are also leaders. The computer can tell you if there is campground space in the area where you want to stay and will give you a printout on how to get to the campground. A friendly staffer at the welcome center is usually on hand to telephone the campground on your behalf to make a reservation.

Choosing a Safe Space

When you get to a campground, you may have to stop at the entrance, where you are assigned a certain space, and that is all there is to it. In many public campgrounds you have a great deal of discretion as to where you camp, for you are usually allowed to drive around the circle road past the various sites and pick the one you want, providing it is unoccupied. Some campers are quick to spot a site with a level pad and attractive surroundings as they mosey along in their rigs; others prefer to leave their RV at the entrance and take a walk through the campground to get a more judicious view of the pluses and minuses that the various sites have to offer.

Whether you select your site on foot or from your RV, keep in mind these safety points: Do not park your rig under a large tree with dead limbs, since a windstorm can bring the branches crashing down on you. You also should avoid the highest point in the area, particularly if you are in the open, because of the danger from lightning. You do not want to camp in a gully, particularly in the Southwest, where flash floods can strike without warning, or beneath an overhanging cliff, where a heavy rain might trigger a rock or mud slide.

These days most RV campsites are reasonably level, and the latest refrigerators are not as sensitive as they used to be. Nevertheless, your first chore once you have pulled into a campsite is to make sure that the bubble in your level is within the circle or your refrigerator cannot operate efficiently and may burn itself out in a vain attempt. Some RVers carry along two boards to place under their wheels to help level the rig.

U.S. campers can discover untrammeled sites sheltered on timber ridges or on the banks of fishing streams such as Telleck Branch and Big River in the Mark Twain National Forest, which sweeps over the Ozark Plateau in Missouri. They can pull their rigs into Custer State Park in South Dakota, where a buffalo herd runs free in a park that is as large and varied as most national parks, and they can camp on the flanks of Mount Rainier, that majestic landmark of the Pacific Northwest. They can park their rigs on a California beach on the sunset edge of the continent or camp in Maine's 200,000-acre Baxter State Park, where Mount Katahdin is the first peak in the United States to be lit by the rising sun.

10
Cooking in an RV

When covered-wagon families, those pioneer RVers, reached the high plains, they found themselves in buffalo chip country. Since there was little wood to be found, they cooked over fires built of the chips. On the Oregon Trail, Emil Conyers noted in his diary, "Many of the ladies can be seen roaming over the prairie with sacks in hand, searching for a few buffalo chips to cook their evening meal. Some of the ladies are seen wearing gloves, but most of them have discarded their gloves and are gathering the buffalo chips with their bare hands."

Cooking Out

At least pioneers discovered that a steak cooked over a buffalo-chip fire required no pepper. Their successors in today's RVs are happy to supply a more orthodox pepper from a shaker and confine their cooking to a microwave oven or perhaps an LP-gas stove. If they

131

decide to cook out, they may prepare their meals over a wood fire at their campsite or take out a charcoal grill or hibachi. Sometimes they cook over a wood fire just for the fun of it. Then they might heed the advice of the Apache chief Lydo Harvey, who showed our camping family how to start a fire in wet weather. He placed all his tinder, kindling, and fuel wood in neat piles within easy reach. Using a crisscross lay, he lit his fire from the windward side. Then he fed the lee of the fire with first the kindling and then larger pieces of wood as his tinder flared up. As for lighting a charcoal fire safely, this has been a backyard U.S. art for several generations now. There is one word of caution: we have seen RVers carry their hibachis indoors when the rain began to fall, without appreciating that burning charcoal consumes oxygen at a rapid rate and can fill an RV with deadly carbon monoxide in no time at all.

Choosing Recipes

Most RV cooks choose their recipes to please the palate, provide balanced nutrition, and take advantage of available foodstuffs that require minimal refrigerator space and are easy to prepare. Some families tend to use microwaves or any other means to cut short the time spent in meal preparation. They favor convenience foods, purchased from supermarkets in the towns they pass through on their way to the camp.

Cooking from Scratch

Still, there is a pronounced backlash against convenience foods and spur-of-the-moment meals among RV travelers, and this includes many families as well as adults who are traveling without children. These stalwarts prefer such things as preparing a stew or baking bread from scratch and stopping in a wild berry patch along the way to pick blackberries for a cobbler served that night for dessert. Many RVers also are discovering the fun of experimenting in regional cuisine as they travel about the country. They may prepare a Boston clam chowder at a Cape Cod campsite or attempt Indian fry bread when camped on South Dakota's Rosebud Oglala Sioux Reservation. Knowing this, the state of Tennessee's computerized welcome centers provide such information as where visitors can pick fruits or vegetables in season or buy them fresh from roadside stands. The computer also furnishes recipes on how to cook the produce on an RV's stove.

RV Cooking Tricks

An experienced RV cook has learned a few tricks. Some small campers have only two burners, so a cook may prepare some things in advance, leaving at least one of the burners available to cook things that need doing at the last minute. Just before serving, the cook can reheat the first dish. Others with limited in-the-rig cooking facilities start a wood or charcoal fire outside the rig to supplement what they can handily prepare on their LP-gas stove.

Some stoves have ovens, with or without temperature gauges, and some rigs contain a microwave where the oven used to be. Some RV cooks count on a deep-well cooker pot to serve as an oven, and others employ a reflector-type oven, either over the stove's burners or out of doors at a campfire. Some RVers also carry along a Dutch oven and a pressure cooker.

When it comes to refrigeration, the ice boxes of

Inside the Kitchen of a Motor Home

the early-day RVs have long since given way to refrigerators, many of which have small freezers to store frozen foods. Typically, the refrigerators work with gas,
110-volt AC, or 12-volt DC. Some make the switch automatically, depending upon which is the most efficient
at the time, but most require that the RVer change the
refrigerator from one power source to another. The refrigerator uses 110-volt AC electricity when the rig is
hooked up in a campsite and 12-volt DC when it is on
the road; it can also depend on the battery. Usually in
camp when there is no hookup, or if the vehicle is

parked for a long time by the road, the refrigerator can be changed to gas. Some RV campers also bring along a cooler with dry ice or ice blocks in it to supplement their refrigerator.

RVers cool only the foods that need refrigeration, keep the others in their cabinets, and open and close the refrigerator as little as possible. They take out and replace all the perishable foods that they use in a meal at the same time.

Utensils for the RV Kitchen

Ideally, RVers will select their cooking equipment carefully and keep it to a minimum. The kitchen can be both efficient and well-stocked if it contains the following utensils.

> nesting pans with lids, one, two, and three quarts in size
> teflon-coated skillet and lid
> plastic microware
> teakettle
> coffee pot
> toaster
> nest of metal bowls for mixing
> assorted cutlery
> service for four people
> can opener
> bottle opener

Living off the Land

Tennessee is scarcely the only state that provides visitors with information on pick-it-yourself produce and regional cuisine. Most state tourist departments will gladly send you information on the subject, but the

most enjoyable experiences are when you just happen
on an orchard full of ripe cherries around Michigan's
Traverse Bay or a roadside stand high in the New Mexico mountains near Cloudcroft selling apples that were
freshly picked from trees along the road. We were roll-
ing down U.S. 92, east of Tampa, and came upon Plant
City when the strawberries were ripe. This self-styled
strawberry capital of the world was celebrating the in-
credible fecundity of its fields. There were hundreds of
passing RVers and other motorists picking their own
strawberries, and the road was lined with stands where
strawberries in six-quart baskets were on sale at prices
that could not be ignored. Dozens of other stands offered freshly baked shortcake, smothered with strawberries, and sundaes made with still more strawberries. Some stands advertised shortcake mixes with
the hope that passing RVs would stop. Very few vehicles managed to pass without stopping. We have never
had more luscious strawberries. They not only graced
our shortcake that night at dinner but added their
sweet goodness to cereal in the morning for the next
several days and served as roadside snacks. A handful
of strawberries, we discovered, makes an excellent
midafternoon pick-me-up for a jaded driver.

On another Florida visit we stopped off at Highlands Hammock State Park and discovered Seville oranges growing wild. A ranger told us that Floridians
make a sour orange pie out of these wild oranges that
rivals the celebrated Key lime pie in excellence. The
pie seems to taste even better when you pick your own
oranges. It tastes better still when you learn that these
oranges were originally planted by Spanish mariners.
What the lime was to the British sailor, the sour Seville
orange was to the Spanish. It came with Columbus to
the New World and sailed with other Spanish ships as
well so that the crews would not get scurvy. Since the

galleons had no refrigeration, the health-giving oranges could only be counted on for perhaps three months before rotting, and the Spanish planted orange seeds wherever they landed. Birds, animals, and possibly Indians carried the fruit inland, where today it grows wild, ready to be made into a tangy marmalade or a pie that is unforgettable. Of course, RVers who visit not only Florida but also the Texas Rio Grande Valley, Arizona, and California discover that the far better known sweet orange is readily available along the road, too, since that day long ago when these oranges were first carried out of their native land of China.

Roadside Wild Foods

America is a vast potpourri of roadside delicacies, some as tame as the sweet orange and some as wild as the Seville orange. The Spanish also sowed mustard greens along El Camino Real on the coast of California, and today's RVers can pick the tender, small leaves of the greens. They can discover wild asparagus from the end of April through early June in such heart-of-America states as Wisconsin, Minnesota, Michigan, Illinois, and Iowa. It grows along fences and in the shade of trees. Wild asparagus fanciers know that they must look for the telltale white tips thrusting up through the grass and leaves. If the plant has gone to flower, the stalk is already too tough.

Roadside fields and forests can also furnish an RVer with the makings of a soup. A mess of watercress, burdock, wild onions, and chopped bacon can be simmered in a pot. Pancakes can be made of the starchy roots of the cattail, mixed with water to make a cake. Most RVers know that the popular staples tomatoes, potatoes, and corn are native North Ameri-

can vegetables, which were domesticated by the
Indians before the vegetables found their way into the
settlers' larders. To this day these vegetables have wild
cousins that can make intriguing additions to an RVer's
diet. Many of the most nutritious wild edible plants
grow in wet places. The arrowhead, also known as the
swamp potato, lifts its dark green leaves, shaped like
arrowheads, and its white flowers near water and
marshes. When autumn comes, tubers form along the
roots. These can be dug up and roasted. The cattail is
still another North American plant that grows close to
streams and swamps. When still green, its head can be
boiled or roasted, much as you would prepare an ear
of corn. You can also eat the roots raw or cooked, and
you can eat the shoots as if they were asparagus. As for
the cattail's pollen, it can be used as a wild flour to
make griddle cakes.

Thousands of other edible wild plants are to be
found in the United States. They include dandelions
and burdock, yellow dock and milkweed, wild grape,
and sunflowers. Sunflower seeds are eaten raw or
roasted, and they can make a conversation-starting
snack at a cocktail party that you may decide to give in
your rig on some rainy afternoon.

The wilderness is home to excellent teas too. Sas-
safras roots and stems sectioned and boiled make a
tea. So will wild rose hips, which furnished Alaska
sourdoughs with Vitamin C. You might wish to brew
sumac, the source of a bracing sour drink that resem-
bles lemonade in taste.

Our Cooking Heritage

The cuisine of every state is part of our common heritage. Throughout the high plains and mountain

states, beef jerky has been popular ever since the Sioux, after removing as much fat as they could, sliced buffalo meat into thin strips. They hung the meat to dry in the sun so that it would last indefinitely on a trip. The pioneers quickly learned about buffalo and then beef jerky. RVers find jerky on sale in convenience stores and supermarkets throughout the West.

A Wyoming cowboy once told us that an Old West cook, whomping up a mess of chow for a gang of hungry cowhands, cooked up the whole beef. He served meat for breakfast, dinner, and supper; he served it fried, boiled, broiled, and stewed. Into his "son-of-a-gun stew" he threw everything—heart and liver, sweetbreads and tongue, even strips of lean steak. Today's RVers are apt to be a little more reserved as to what meats they toss in the pot, but they, too, whomp up what they call a chuck wagon mulligan.

Everybody knows that the fertile fields of the Pennsylvania Dutch country provide travelers with fabulous fare and that Amish and Mennonite recipes are "wonderful good." There also are Mennonite and Amish settlements in Ohio, Indiana, Illinois, Iowa, and South Dakota—to name only a few states. A *schmeckfest* at Freeman, South Dakota, is as much a *schmeckfest* as one held in Lancaster County, Pennsylvania. Such dishes as *dampffleish* (stewed beef), *bratwurst* (pork sausage), *nudel suppe* (noodle soup), *grüne schauble suppe* (green bean soup), *dicke bohnen* (navy beans with ham), and *käse mit knoft* (coffee cake) are prepared. Every year 2,000 schmeckfest banqueters at Freeman devour 470 pounds of sausage, 900 pounds of beef, 170 gallons of soup, 410 pounds of potatoes, and 48 gallons of sauerkraut, which led one visiting RVer to observe, "Now I know why they call it the schmeckfest. When I came in and smelled the delicious food, I 'schmecked' my lips. Now I'm so full I can't button my 'fvest.' "

An RVer can take along the recipes gladly offered by the hospitable Plain Dutch people and try them out later on. In the same friendly way, a Maine coaster will teach a visitor how to dig for clams and cook them and will also demonstrate exactly how to cook beans in a hole in the ground filled with hot coals and covered with dirt. Lobster in New England, trout in Wyoming, shrimp in Georgia, catfish in Missouri, salmon steak in Washington and Oregon and Alaska, and crayfish in the Cajun country of Louisiana are just a few regional foods that can add a special delight to an RV journey.

In the Louisiana bayou country west of New Orleans, Cajun children wade in ponds in search of crayfish. Joan and I stopped to photograph two youngsters and soon found ourselves wading in the ponds too. The kids invited us to their nearby home, where their mother had a pot of crayfish bisque on the stove. She offered us a cup, and it was as delectable a soup as we ever tasted. The best source of recipes for use in your rig is the people you meet as you travel around the country. Perhaps the second best source is the chef in a restaurant where you particularly enjoy a regional dish.

In Kentucky, hound dogs followed Wallace Potts's truck as he moseyed down the roads near Georgetown.

"They're getting in a good sniff as they go," Potts told us. His truck was redolent of beef basted in savory juices over hardwood coals and beans cooked in lard cans over open fires, and the dogs could scarcely be blamed for their twitching noses. A Kentucky burgoo festival is a culinary spectacle, as pleasing to the eye as it is to the stomach.

As RVers travel through the South and Southwest in fall, fleeing the snows of the North, they should keep their noses as alert as a hound dog's for possible good eating. They might find wild duck roasting amid the rice fields near Stuttgart, Arkansas; a pig turning on a spit in a churchyard in Alabama; or potatoes boiling in resin in the piney woods of Georgia. They might share in a pot of simmering chili at a Texas county fair or eat Indian pan bread right out of a beehive oven at a New Mexico pueblo.

All over the South you will find spoon bread, fried corn, hominy, grits, corn pone, and hush puppies, and you can prepare them all in your rig. The South is also the home of country-fried steak and fried chicken, tasty and juicy if prepared by a master of the art. Pecan pie is universal in the South, too, though you will find Atlanta, Birmingham, and Nashville all claiming to serve the best slice. Probably the most argued-about dish in the South is ham. Even Virginians, who agree on most things, quarrel when it comes to ham. Country hams are the pride of the Piedmont and the Blue Ridge, and Smithfield hams are the pride of the Tidewater.

Maple syrup in Vermont; pancakes on Shrove Tuesday in Liberal, Kansas, when women run a 415-yard S-shaped course, flipping their cakes as they compete with the women in Olney, England, who are running an identical course; Swiss cheese bought right from a Monroe, Wisconsin, cheese maker; a flaky Cornish pasty in the Upper Peninsula of Michigan mining country; sawmill gravy (a milk gravy with bits of sausage) in the mountains of eastern Tennessee; or even cactus to munch on in the Arizona desert—all appeal to the taste buds. Chewing on a cactus might not be every RVer's idea of how to pamper the stomach, but the prickly pear cactus is a versatile food. The flat leaf, stripped of its spines, is sold fresh or in cans as a gourmet snack, and the purplish fruit can be eaten raw or made into jam and candy. The fruit of the saguaro can be made into wine.

Everywhere you travel in the United States and across the borders in Canada and Mexico, there is good food. About much of it you can quote Mark Twain on pompano prepared by the Creoles of New Orleans: "It is as delicious as the less criminal forms of sin." Sampled at festivals or in restaurants along the road and then prepared at your pleasure in your own recreation vehicle, the inexhaustible variety of regional cuisine adds savor to an RVer's life.

11
Campground Neighbors and Club Friends

RVers like to think of themselves as good neighbors on wheels, and it is true that the recreation vehicle life-style lends itself to long-lasting friendships. People who happen to camp next to one another for a few days usually discover that an exchange of addresses and phone numbers really has meaning and that they are likely to see their friends of a night or two in a campground again, perhaps halfway across the country. This is particularly true of retired RVers who cultivate a talent for friendship.

Good Campground Neighbors

RVers soon discover that they are expected to be good campground neighbors. Some campgrounds post a set of rules for you to see when you check in, but others count on your basic good manners or your knowledge of campground courtesy. Campground etiquette simply reflects common sense.

You do not play a radio, a tape deck, or a phonograph loudly at any time in a campground. Barking dogs are not appreciated either. As far as that goes, only well-behaved and sociable dogs are appreciated in campgrounds, and a snarling pet is going to make other campers glad to see you move on. Nor should dogs run loose or foul the campground. Some campgrounds do not even allow dogs, so it is a good idea for a dog owner to learn what the policy is before making a reservation.

Generators muttering away at night also upset the campground calm. When dusk draws near, people with good camping manners turn their generators off and run their rigs off the 110-volt hookup or with gas. When there are no hookups, most RVers need the generator to provide power for their air conditioners and microwave ovens. A thoughtful camper makes absolutely certain that the night really is so sultry that an air conditioner is necessary, since, with or without the generator, it makes an annoying hum that can interfere with the sleep of the occupants of other RVs, let alone the tent campers. Bright gas lanterns hiss, and they should be turned off when sleep time arrives. If you stay up late at night to play cards or simply to talk with your friends, be thoughtful of early retirers. In turn, they will be expected to be thoughtful of late risers when they get up at dawn to go fishing or saunter off on an early morning bird hike.

RVers pride themselves in living by the outdoors code, and this means that when they check into a campsite, they invariably pick up any litter that a less-experienced camper may have left in their site. They keep their site tidy and make sure that when they depart, they leave it cleaner than when they found it. They make sure that they put their refuse in the containers provided for the purpose and, above all, avoid contaminating any lake or stream. Some people who fish claim that it does not matter if they clean their fish in a lake, but they probably will have a hard time convincing their campground neighbors that they are not just being thoughtless.

A Club for Every RVer

The interest of RVers in joining clubs springs from the same source as their interest in cultivating friendships and their concern for being good neighbors. Camping clubs may be made up of people who own a certain make of RV or a certain type of RV or who have a certain interest. (A listing of brand-name and national RV clubs is given in Appendix E.) The Frustrated Maestros are a division of the Family Motor Coach Association that is made up of people who play homemade musical instruments, such as washboards and kazoos. Most people enjoy having these amateur musicians put on an impromptu concert at the campsite, but others hope that they might consider camping the next night at least one county away. Groups exist for the handicapped as well as for skiers, ham radio operators, painters, bird-watchers, and people with scores of other interests.

One group is for people who are single. Loners on Wheels, based at Concord, California, has about 3,400 members and thirty chapters throughout the nation made up entirely of single retirees. Members hold annual conventions, regional rallies, and campouts for sociability's sake. They also get together for cookouts, fishing, cards, and talk that never seems to grow stale.

There are even opportunities for RVers to participate in Elderhostel programs. They do not live in dormitories at participating educational institutions as do most Elderhostelers but park their RVs on the campus. Some host institutions provide water and electrical hookups, while others require the RV Elderhostelers to have self-contained units. If there is no space on the campus for an RV camp, provision is made at a nearby state park or private campground. A shuttle bus brings the RV Elderhostelers to the campus for classes and activities.

What Clubs Offer

Many RVers are members of the thirty-four national RV clubs, which, taken all together, have thousands of local and regional chapters. The Good Sam Club alone has 500,000 members. For a nominal fee, clubs offer such things as travel planning, newsletters or magazines, membership lists, chapter and national meetings, and useful information on packing an RV, menu planning, and vehicle maintenance and repairs. Clubs also may forward mail, provide an emergency telephone-message service, enable members to order traveler's checks by mail, provide credit cards, sell insurance, supply road service, and provide discounts on campground fees and gasoline purchases. Good Sam registers keys so that if you lose them and they are found, they will be forwarded to Good Sam headquarters. This club also registers your pets. If your pet is wearing a Good Sam metal tag when it strays, anybody finding it need only call a toll-free number and the club goes to work bringing the lost pet and its owners together again. Above all, clubs provide opportunities for friendship through campouts, rallies, and caravans.

Not everybody enjoys all the aspects of club life. Some people like the comradery and friendship but find that the fun and games at a rally are not for them. They soon discover that most club members respect their privacy and individualism and do not necessarily expect that they will participate in the horseshoe pitching tournament, volleyball game, or pizza party, which others enjoy. Still, campers who have shared a campground with a group called the Chattanooga Choo-Choos find themselves wondering about their sanity. The members put high-fidelity tapes of train whistles in their vehicles and play them at night so that it sounds to their neighbors as though they are camped next to a railroad track.

Club Rallies and Caravans

When several hundred or even several thousand members of an RV club hold a rally, they take over a vast tract. At these gigantic meets, sanitation becomes a

An RV Rally

problem, since there are no sewage hookups available. Sometimes permission is given by the club authorities to dig a series of gopher holes, one for each rig. A tractor equipped with a telephone-pole digger is given the task. When a rig gets ready to leave, it is considered proper for participants to insert a circular board in the hole and cover it with earth so that future campers will not put a foot in it. To make doubly sure that this does not happen, some campers place warning signs over their gopher holes, and some decorate the hole with such things as a miniature outhouse replete with a miniature Sears Roebuck catalog. One rally of the Holiday Rambler Recreational Vehicle Club ended with so many imaginative gopher hole decorations that photographers went about preserving them for posterity. This naturally led to a photographic contest for gopher hole art.

    A club caravan is something to behold. When the

An RV Caravan

Airstreamers take to the road, their wagon master, or caravan leader, stays in touch with the other rigs by CB radio. Because of safety considerations and traffic, a caravan of RVs rarely travels one after the other in something of a convoy, so radio communication is important. At a given moment the members of the caravan could be scattered halfway across a state. There are committees to oversee everything from parking to water and sanitation, and when the trailers come swinging up to a nightly camp, they are parked with a precision that would do the army credit. Since a wagon master must be a consummate diplomat as well as some-time disciplinarian, it is not surprising that most clubs train their wagon masters. Some could have led a covered-wagon trek over the pioneer Oregon Trail and served with distinction.

In the summer of 1984, the RV Executive Council on Foreign Diplomats demonstrated that travel in an RV was also an appealing way for foreigners to see the United States. Every morning with Wagon Master Ellen Stoutenberg, who founded the Executive Council on Foreign Diplomats, in charge, diplomats and their families stationed in Washington and at the United Nations put their rigs in line behind the motor home of an intrepid New Zealander and set out on a day's journey. The international odyssey gave the foreign visitors a candid look at the country, which deepened their appreciation of its people and its vast coast-to-coast sweep. Most of these sophisticated foreigners regretted the end of the caravan trek. Most were converts to the RV way of travel.

12
RV Travel Outside the USA

Cornelius Vanderbilt, Jr., shipped his Halsco Land Yacht to England in 1936 and lived in it when he attended the coronation of King George VI. This pioneer American RV tourist abroad raised a few British eyebrows. When the festivities were over, Vanderbilt toured Britain with his elegant trailer and then took it to the European continent for an extended RV camping trip through fourteen nations. After he returned home and wrote about his journey, other American RVers put their rigs aboard trans-Atlantic liners and set off on their own European jaunts. American RVers were already touring Canada and Mexico, but Europe was another matter.

At first American RVers brought their rigs abroad with them, but they soon found out that pulling a jumbo-sized trailer through the narrow streets of a European village or along a twisting European road was more than they had bargained for. With the expansion of air transportation in the years following World War II, it also became increasingly costly to

ship a rig to Europe or other overseas destination by
sea. Today most American RV tourists traveling
abroad rent smaller European vehicles once they have
crossed the ocean.

Caravans in Europe

British eyebrows may have been raised at Vanderbilt's
trailer, but the British recognize a good thing when
they see it! Within a few years "caravans," as the British call RVs, became popular in the British Isles. Unlike U.S. RVers, most of whom buy their RVs, the
British prefer to rent their rigs, and it is in a rented caravan that most people in Britain and on the European
continent go caravanning.

On recent trips to Britain, my wife and I have
marveled at the omnipresent mini motor homes and
trailers that fill campgrounds. They turned up beside a
Scottish loch, tucked into a castle courtyard in north
England for the night, or ensconced in romantic solitude on the rocky coast of Northern Ireland, where the
occupants were studying bird life. Most of these caravanners were British, but among them we found
North Americans who are discovering that RVing on
the far side of the Atlantic brings them as close to the
people and to the land as it does in North America.
Similarly, we have seen caravanners parked in the virtually unknown national parks of northern Portugal,
winding through the Bavarian Alps, trekking among
the chateaux on the French Loire, and exploring the
northern Greek province of Macedonia. One American family we encountered in Macedonia had been in-
spired by the Alexander the Great exhibit that the
University of Thessaloniki had sent to the United
States and was camping its way from one archaeolog-

ical site related to Alexander to another. (For information on Austria, Belgium, Cyprus, Denmark, Finland, France, Germany, Great Britain, Greece, Iceland, Ireland, Italy, Luxembourg, Malta, Monaco, Netherlands, Norway, Portugal, Spain, Sweden, Switzerland, Turkey, and Yugoslavia, contact the European Travel Commission, 630 Fifth Avenue, Suite 611, New York, NY 10111, 212-307-1200.)

Renting an RV Abroad

Several of the international airlines can help their passengers rent RVs in Europe or elsewhere in the world. Lufthansa is particularly capable of providing a fly-and-drive service. A knowledgeable travel agent can also help with overseas RV rentals through such firms as InterRent, Kemwel, Auto Europe, Europe by Car, Foremost EuroCar, Europacar Tours, and Maiellano Tours. An agent should also be familiar with the major Canadian and U.S. concerns that offer RV rentals not only in Europe but also in Australia and New Zealand, where caravans and campgrounds are common. One of these Canadian operators, Go Vacations, headquartered at Rexdale, Ontario, close to Toronto's airport, offers RV rentals at twenty-two locations in North America and forty-one in Europe, Australia, and New Zealand. In Canada this concern offers primarily Canadian-made vehicles, and in Europe it offers the Bedford, which is a British RV, ideally suited for European travel conditions.

Some Americans take a lesson from Australian and New Zealander RVers when they visit Europe. They find that they save a lot of money by buying a used caravan in London, taking it on their European tour, and then reselling it in London to the next would-be RV tourist. For years the market for used RVs was conveniently located in front of London's Australia House, but now it has moved across the Thames near the Hungerford Bridge. One American couple from Ohio whom we met in London had bought and sold one of these vehicles and found that they had a month's use of it for nothing, since they had actually sold it to a family from South Africa for more than they had paid for it.

"These RVs are just right for the European continent," another American informed us. "They are retired Dutch postal vans, fitted out by a man from Australia. They have turned into big business."

The Economical Way to Go

RV travel abroad not only gives a person a closer look at the nations visited but also is a very economical way to go. The cost of round-trip air travel aside, RV travel overseas is cheaper than staying in hotels and eating in restaurants and less expensive than RV travel in the United States and Canada. There are campgrounds throughout Europe, and most of them have water and electricity hookups. Few have sanitary hookups, though most campgrounds have central washrooms, almost invariably well kept.

Overseas Club Trips

Because many Americans still prefer to travel abroad in RV groups, several RV clubs sponsor overseas RV tours. The Wally Byam Caravan Club International (WBCCI) overseas caravans, as befits the legacy of its peripatetic founder, offers some of the most challenging trips. Recently the club sponsored a four-month trip for twenty families through the British Isles and several north European countries, including all of Scandinavia, with a side trip on a cruise ship from Helsinki, Finland, to Leningrad, Russia. The group landed at Amsterdam and then traveled to Weidenbruk, Germany, to pick up new Volkswagen Vanagon Campers. Another still more adventurous WBCCI caravan set off to tour fifteen countries in Europe and North Africa and ended up in Turkey, in Asia Minor. The caravanners began their journey at Osnabrück, Germany, where they attended a meeting of the German branch of the International Camper Association. On both of these tours, camping families were able to purchase the Vanagon Campers at a greatly reduced price, which included the cost of shipping the vehicle to an American seaport. The Good Sam Club also sponsors what it calls Caraventures through Europe.

Probably the most adventurous of all RV trips carried out in recent years was also sponsored by the WBCCI. It was the idea of Frank Sargent, a retired engineer living in Fort Myers, Florida, who with his wife, Vivian, had been a camper for twenty years. They had already traveled in twenty-six foreign countries. It was their idea to take a tour group to China. After considerable negotiation with the Chinese government, a satisfactory agreement was reached. Sargent also persuaded the Airstream Corporation to construct and equip trailers especially designed for Chinese roads, which range from modern concrete highways to endless dirt tracks and ancient surfaces paved with enormous blocks of stone. General Motors Truck and Coach Division built the tow vehicles. In July 1985, the rigs were shipped to China by sea. On September 2, ten American retired couples, whose average age was seventy, arrived at the Port of Xiamen by air and met the vehicles. After a tour all over China, the dauntless RVers flew home. The vehicles remained behind to be used by groups of caravanners from America through the spring of 1987 and then given, with all they contain, to the people of China.

An RV trip through Europe, through the lands down under, or to China appeals to the adventurous, but Canada and Mexico are far and away the most popular destinations outside the United States. Baja California never seems to lose its appeal to West Coast RV campers, and there are large colonies of RV full-timers, not only in Mexico but also in Costa Rica, far to the south. So many U.S. and Canadian RVers, augmented by a strong contingent from Great Britain and Australia, attended the Vancouver World's Fair in 1986 that special campgrounds had to be built for them.

Visiting Canada in an RV

Most Americans scarcely think they are leaving their own nation when they visit their neighbor to the north. Canada's common heritage with the United States and the generations-old friendship that binds the two nations together make this seem a logical destination for RV travelers. In addition, Canada has superb national and provincial parks, where an RV camper can experience everything from a midnight serenade by a pack of wolves to a carefree game of golf.

Still, Canada is a foreign country, and its exceedingly polite and friendly border authorities are exceedingly strict. To visit Canada, a native-born U.S. citizen should have proof of citizenship, either a birth or baptismal certificate or a voting registration card. If you have a passport, it is certainly a good idea to take it along, but it is not essential. A naturalized U.S. citizen should carry a naturalization certificate or passport. A foreign national residing in the United States should take not only a passport but also an Alien Registration Receipt Card. The U.S. Immigration Service will want to see these documents on your return to the United States. Anybody younger than eighteen who is not accompanied by an adult should bring along a letter from a parent or guardian giving the individual permission to travel in Canada. Pets should be declared at the border. A dog or cat will be allowed to visit Canada, providing it has a rabies vaccination certificate not more than three years old. Take the certificate with you, and be sure it bears a "legible and adequate description" of the pet.

You will also need a valid driver's license, and you should ask your insurance agent for a Non-Resident Inter-Provinces Motor Vehicle Liability Insurance Card. If you are driving a rented RV, you must have the vehicle registration form with you. In case you have borrowed the vehicle from a friend or a member of your family, you should take along a letter from its owner saying that you have permission to drive it into Canada. The Canadians also take into account that you may want to leave a travel trailer in their country for a season while you return home from time to time. When you check through Canadian Customs, ask for a wallet-sized E-99 permit, which you should post in your trailer in such a way that it can be seen from the outside. You need not hand the permit back at the end of the season but may use it again next year, providing it has not expired. The Canadians, however, do not allow U.S. citizens to store their travel trailers in their country during the winter season. You can keep your RV in Canada up to twelve months, and you need not leave the country where you entered it.

At one time Canada required travelers to register their citizens band radios when they entered the country, but this is no longer so. Permits for a citizens band radio up to 100 milliwatts operating on the 26.9–27.27 megahertz band are no longer required of visitors to the country, but these radios must be registered in the United States. Other types of radio equipment may be sealed at the border, and if you break the seal during your Canadian sojourn, you may not take the radio out of the country.

Canadian customs personnel rarely check out your food stocks aboard, but technically speaking, you are not supposed to bring more than two days' food into the country. Fresh fruit is not admitted into Canada. If you have a freezer aboard filled with meat, this would be a clear violation of the law and could cause you difficulty. Far more important, you must not bring handguns into Canada. One caravan of RVs was held up for hours at the border in 1985 when authorities discovered a single handgun in one of the vehicles.

"We do not want Saturday night specials in this country," warns Alec Carman of Tourism Canada in Ottawa, who, among other things, helps foreign visitors who have trouble with Canadian regulations. "You won't need a handgun here anyway. Charges can be serious."

Carman also adds, "Long guns are okay. They may be imported into Canada without a permit, providing the visitor is sixteen years of age or over and the hunting rifle or shotgun is for sporting or competition use. You must be sure to declare the gun, however."

He also advises RV travelers to be open when declaring what liquors they have aboard. "It is easy to forget the bottle of wine in the refrigerator," he admits, and quickly adds, "but don't forget it."

Carman advises that RV travelers make a mental

Stop

No left turn

Railway
advance
warning

Yield

Narrow
structure

Drive
on right

Children
at play

Sharp
turn

School

Right
turn

Winding
road

One way

100 km/h
(60 mph)
Major
highways

80 km/h
(50 mph)
Rural
highways

50 km/h
(30 mph)
Cities

Canadian Traffic Signs

check on what they have aboard before they come to the Canadian border so that they know what they have to declare. Experienced RVers know that they should exchange their currency after they cross the Canadian border in order to get the best rate. Some tourists continue to shop with their U.S. dollars when visiting their northern neighbor and count on Canadian businesses to give them the correct discount. They usually will obtain a much better rate by going to a currency exchange or bank. Most U.S. bank credit cards are accepted in Canada.

Additional information on visiting Canada can be obtained from provincial and territorial tourist offices. See Appendix F for a list of addresses.

Canadian Friendliness

Once you have crossed the border into Canada, you will find yourselves in a country that is known all over the world for its open-hearted friendliness. Official Canada is just as friendly as the people you will meet in towns and on farms. Parks Canada, in Ottawa, is ready to help you plan your trip providing you let them know what part of the enormous continental nation you want to visit. Be specific, and Parks Canada will send you regional guides. Excellent literature about the individual parks can be obtained at the visitor reception centers.

You may decide to do all your camping in national or provincial parks, but Canada also has a well-developed array of private campgrounds and a surprising number of municipal campgrounds. You may bring back happy camping memories from such renowned places as Banff or Jasper in the West or Algonquin Provincial Park in Ontario, but you would do well to include in your camping adventures a stay in such unknown places as the municipal campground at Napean, an Ontario town only ten miles from Ottawa, Canada's national capital and one of the continent's fascinating cities.

Visiting Mexico in an RV

Mexico is as close to the United States as is Canada. The Mexican nation is the enduring child of two civilizations. The stones of the Cathedral of Mexico City were cut long before the Spaniards came to the New World. They were once part of the towering Aztec temple to the sun. Cortez's soldiers pulled down the temple and used its stone to erect a temple to the Christian God. In this way they built a nation upon ancient Indian foundations. Today's Mexico proudly traces its beginnings to the Mayas, Toltecs, and Aztecs and to the Spanish Conquistadores. Mexico is a hospitable land that lies to the sunny south of English-speaking North America, and it is one of the most colorful countries in the world.

Some North Americans do not consider Mexico friendly. They read newspaper headlines of drug smugglers, political corruption, police brutality, and bandits who prey on motorists, and they decide that, colorful country or not, they have no intention of visiting Mexico. The truth is that although Mexico has developed more than its share of problems, RV tourists are very welcome and almost always safe. They should, however, take certain precautions to avoid having unnecessary trouble.

Just as it is important to meet Canadian entrance regulations, it is necessary to meet Mexican requirements. Tourists traveling into Mexico must have a tourist card, which can be picked up at the border crossing point or in advance at a Mexican consulate or tourist office. A U.S. citizen needs only to prove citizenship to receive the card. A person under eighteen years of age, however, who is not traveling with parents must carry a notarized affidavit granting permission to travel into Mexico, signed by both of the parents or guardians. If a mother or father decides to visit Mexico with a child under eighteen, the other parent must sign a notarized affidavit giving permission. As for cats and dogs, they may cross the border providing their owners have obtained a permit from a Mexican consulate. It is necessary to present a current vaccination and health certificate from a veterinarian to obtain the permit.

To bring an RV, or for that matter any other vehicle, into Mexico, an owner must obtain a combination tourist card and temporary vehicle-import permit. Once you have filled in the personal part of the permit with the help of the immigration official, you take it to the customs official. You must bring along your title or registration so that the official can complete the vehicular part of the form. Both the personal and vehicular parts of the form are good for up to six months. It is critical that the two sections of the form agree as to the date of expiration. If for some reason you decide to leave the RV in Mexico to make a return trip into the United States, you must leave the vehicle at the nearest government office that will accept it. There it may remain without question for six months. After an additional grace period of forty-five days, it will be confiscated by the Mexican Treasury Department.

Mexican law also requires that you buy Mexican insurance. Your U.S. insurance is not valid in Mexico, and foreign adjusters are not allowed to make settlements or adjustments in that country. You must buy Mexican insurance before you cross the border. Rates are regulated by the Mexican government, so the costs are the same wherever the policy is written. Above all, do not attempt to take your RV into Mexico without Mexican insurance or, even if you have only a slight accident, you may well end up in jail.

The Mexican government allows CB radios into the country without permits, but RVers are asked to avoid using them in cities or towns, where they may interfere with police and other transmissions, which are often on the same bands. Mexican authorities allow visitors to bring in sports firearms providing they have obtained a firearms certificate from a consular office. Once in Mexico, you must apply to the proper military authorities for a temporary permit, valid for ninety days, which enables you to carry the weapons.

It is a good idea to talk with Mexican tourist office personnel before making your trip to learn what the rules are concerning duty-free limits. To the surprise of many an RV traveler, some things carried aboard their rigs may well be dutiable. Some jewelry, machinery, antiques, and biological materials are subject to a tax, to name a few categories that you should think about. If there is any question, leave the item at home. (Sources for general travel information and for answers to specific questions about travel in Mexico are given in Appendix G.)

Safety in Mexico

There are other things to think about when RV traveling in Mexico. The very pavements are more abrasive than those in the United States, and they have chuckholes where you least expect them. This can be hard on your tires and your disposition. The condition

of the roads is a good reason to keep your rig down to
the sixty-miles-per-hour speed limit on the road and
the twenty-five-miles-per-hour limit in the towns.
North Americans who have grown accustomed to motorists blinking their lights politely to show that they
plan to turn right or left soon discover that Mexican
drivers suddenly veer one way or the other without any
warning signal. There is also a "moment of truth"
every time you come to a one-way bridge. You are expected to yield the right of way to a commercial vehicle, especially if it is bigger than your rig is, and you
must defer to any driver who manages to flash lights
before you do. It scarcely needs saying that RV travelers should avoid driving at night, when a collision
with a wandering cow can involve them in all kinds of
controversy. Certainly it is a good idea to have your rig
parked snug and safe in a campground by dark. Do not
leave it on a town street overnight, or for that matter,
do not leave it unattended during the day. You can pay
someone a few pesos to keep an eye on it for you.

Caravans to Mexico

Considering all the problems that RV travel in Mexico
can occasion, it may be a good idea to make your first
trip to that fascinating country as part of a caravan. A
number of these, including the Sundance Cruises of
Seattle, carry RVs and their passengers alike down the
west coast of Mexico.

"In the words of the RVers," claims Sundance
Cruises' Gordon Thorne, "our ship has been a 'god-
send' for them, allowing them to avoid the long trip
down over less than well-maintained roads. Most of
the Americans we're now transporting are people who
vacation in Mexico all winter; they will return with us

in late March or April. And in addition to taking their vehicles, we also allow them to take their dogs or cats with them. The animals stay in the RV, and the owners are allowed on the car deck four times a day to walk, water, and feed them."

Other tours into Mexico take a piggyback train ride over the Chihuahua al Pacifico Railroad from Chihuahua City through the spectacular Sierra Madre to Topolobampo on the Gulf of California. With experienced tour leaders such as Larry and Maria Olsen of El Paso, Texas, who have been taking their "Tracks to Adventure" (2811 Jackson, Suite E, El Paso, TX 79930, 915-565-9627) RV caravans south of the border for a number of years, a lot of the hassle inherent in Mexican travel can be eliminated.

Visiting Central America

Until the political turmoil in Nicaragua and countries surrounding it, many RV caravans sponsored by RV clubs regularly journeyed all the way to Panama. Today the only Central American country that is popular with RVers is Costa Rica, a secure democracy where law and order are the rule. There are some 30,000 retired Americans living in Costa Rica, and many of them have RVs. Since an individual can take an RV into Costa Rica every five years without paying tax, many Americans living in the country do exactly that. At the end of five years, they can sell the vehicle for as much or more than they paid for it in the United States. Costa Rica may not be as fascinating a country as Mexico, but its security gives it an appeal to retired people who want a Latin American ambience without problems.

Whether you visit a neighboring country or journey halfway across the world, you most likely will have uptight moments, but the pleasures, the adventures, and the new insights far outweigh any difficulties that may occur.

Metric to English Speed Conversions

Metric (kilometers per hour)	*equal approximately*	*English* (miles per hour)
25 KPH		15 MPH
40 KPH		25 MPH
50 KPH		30 MPH
60 KPH		37 MPH
80 KPH		50 MPH
100 KPH		60 MPH

13
RVs in Winter

RV snowbirds winging southward to Texas's Rio Grande Valley and to Arizona's Valley of the Sun to escape the northern winter often meet southern snow addicts driving north in their RVs to the ski slopes of Colorado. It used to be that RVers who could not drive south for the winter stored their vehicles until the spring. Now so many RVers are showing up at New England, Michigan, and western ski resorts that some motels and resorts provide electrical connections for them. Many northern campgrounds remain open all year. Ice fishing enthusiasts also have discovered that a shack out on the ice may be just fine when the fish are biting, but when it comes time to settle down for a night's slumber, there is nothing like an RV waiting on a nearby shore with all the comforts of home. Other snow lovers, with their snowmobiles snugged on trailers tagging along behind their motor homes, head for wintry forest trails for a weekend of adventure. Still other northern RVers use their rigs to go to football games.

Winterizing an RV

Whether you store your RV for the winter or continue to travel in it despite the snow and ice, there are a number of things you have to do to winterize it. The National Safety Council urges you to make sure that your furnace is in good condition if you plan to use your RV in the winter. On a cold winter's night your heater can get a real workout, and you do not want it to conk out just when you need it the most. Some RVers use butane gas as well as propane gas to fuel their ovens, hot-water heaters, furnaces, and refrigerators. If the temperature reaches freezing, butane will not vaporize, and since it is the vapor that operates your RV heating system and your refrigerator, you are in trouble. Be sure that your LP-gas tank is filled with propane, which will vaporize down to forty-four degrees Fahrenheit below zero, and be sure it is filled all the way. On a long weekend when there is a cold snap, you may burn forty pounds of LP gas and think nothing of it. For this reason some RVers obtain oversized LP-gas tanks if they are going to use their rigs in the winter.

Sometimes a gas regulator will freeze up and prevent gas from leaving the tank.

"Thaw a frozen regulator by pouring boiling water over it," urges the National Safety Council. "Never use a flame."

For safety's sake it is also important to leave a vent open when you are using your furnace or any gas-burning appliance to prevent carbon monoxide from building up in your rig. If you find that your furnace is not able to keep your RV warm, you may want to supplement its heat with a fourteen-ampere or smaller electric heater, but do not risk using your cooking stove or a catalytic heater.

Both your owner's manual and your dealer can

provide helpful information on the use of your vehicle's waste, water, and heating systems in the winter. You will want to pay attention to the condition of your tires, electrical system, and any other automotive equipment that may take a beating in the cold. Be sure to add antifreeze to your engine to protect it well below the temperature you reasonably expect, and take along an extra container of antifreeze just in case.

A Winter RV Trip

A winter RV trip calls for the same detailed planning that you would give to a summer trip, but you should be even more certain that you have done your homework. Since not all campgrounds are open in winter, you will want to make sure that you have a reservation where you plan to stop. An electrical hookup is particularly valuable in the winter, and you should confirm that you will have it available.

A frozen water line is one of the chronic problems of RV winter camping. You may wrap your hoses with heat tape, but this will not do you much good if the mercury falls to the bottom of the thermometer. For this reason most RVers completely drain their water systems for the winter and take along portable water containers on cold season trips. You can use the water from the containers for cooking and flushing the toilet, providing you have put RV antifreeze in the holding tanks. Since the drain lines beneath your vehicle freeze first, you have to protect these by adding antifreeze at the first hint of frost in the air. Cover your dump valves with plastic to keep them from freezing shut. If a dump valve does freeze or get covered with snow, thaw it out by pouring warm water over it. Do not attempt to free it with brute strength; you are likely to snap it off in the chill.

Winter Driving

Driving a motor home or towing a trailer on icy roads requires skill and a certain amount of determination. Keep your speed down. From time to time, when no other vehicles are likely to get in your way, check the "feel" of the road by gently applying your brakes and accelerating. Sometimes ice can form on what seems to the eye to be dry pavement, and with your heavy motor home or your trailer behind you, you cannot afford to skid. Be especially cautious on curves; keep your vehicle moving steadily and give other vehicles plenty of room.

Jean-Paul Luc, the famed French driver who heads the Ice Driving School sponsored by Ford and Michelin in Steamboat Springs, Colorado, explains, "To maintain control of your vehicle, the tires must grip the road, and not spin or slide. In winter that means avoiding sudden acceleration, braking, or change of direction. Any time you change the speed or direction of your vehicle, you change the load on the tires. On ice or snow, that can mean a loss of control if you are not prepared to respond properly."

Luc recommends these responses to winter driving problems.

- Sudden stops. Instead of pushing the brake down and holding it, pump the brake pedal repeatedly. This will minimize the braking distance without causing the brakes to "lock," which can result in a loss of vehicle control.
- Rear-wheel skid. If the rear of the vehicle begins to slide, turn the steering wheel in the direction the rear of the vehicle is sliding and accelerate smoothly, avoiding wheel spin. Avoid braking until the skid is corrected.

- Front-wheel skid. If the front of the vehicle begins to slide in a turn, avoid the natural reaction of turning the wheels more in the direction you want to go. Instead, let up on the accelerator and decrease the angle of the turn until the skid is corrected.

You may never need them, but it is a good idea to bring along an ice scraper and a spray deicer as well as chains, a shovel, and dry sand or salt in case you run into a heavy snowfall. Just in case you do encounter a blizzard, stop and stay with your camper. Open a window a crack when you use your heater and count upon exercise to keep warm. Carry along plenty of warm clothing.

A Cold-Weather Campsite

In the summer you may prefer camping high on a windy hill, where the view is sublime, but in the winter you will want to take a lesson from an experienced tent camper and find a sunny spot protected by a windbreak of trees or a hillside. Park with either your rig's rear or its front to the wind to minimize the wind's effect. If the wind can get at your broadside, it may not overturn you, but it certainly will lower the temperature in your RV in a hurry.

Storing an RV for the Winter

Storing your RV for the winter can be simple. Most RVers work from a checklist of things that need doing. They clean the refrigerator, prop its door open, and leave an opened box of baking soda inside to head off any odors. They remove the dry-cell battery if their unit has an electric spark ignitor. They also cover all external vents to the RV to keep out such visitors as mice and squirrels. They close the drapes tightly or decide that the time has come to have them cleaned. They block their trailer up on jacks to keep the tires from deteriorating, and they may cover them to keep the sun's ultraviolet rays from rotting the tire walls.

Here is a list of other things to do, suggested by the Recreation Vehicle Industry Association.

- Drain thoroughly the water storage tank and the piping.
- Drain the hot-water heater.
- Tape the furnace vent closed.
- Disconnect and remove the electric water pump.
- Depress the pedal of the toilet and drain all the water.
- Pour antifreeze down the sink trap.
- Clean the refrigerator and leave it open.
- Drain the holding tank and leave it open.
- Tape the stove vent closed.
- Pour antifreeze down the trap in the shower and washbowl.
- Cover the regulator of the built-in LP tank.
- Close all drapes.
- Clean the filters and cover the air conditioner.
- Keep up the water level and the battery charge.
- Put the unit up on blocks and cover the tires.
- Run the vehicle's engine at least once a month so that it does not deteriorate.

Finally the day will come when you want to take your RV out of wraps and head again for the open road. All you need do is reverse some of the procedures, and you will be set for another season of RV travel. In no time at all you will be on the road again in your RV.

Appendixes

Appendix A

RV Rental Sources

Recreation Vehicle Rental Association
3251 Old Lee Highway, Suite 500
Fairfax, VA 22030
703-591-7130
   (A directory compiled by the RVRA with over 250 listings
of RV dealers who rent RVs costs $4.00 prepaid. There are both
national and Canadian listings.)

Altman's America
1155 Baldwin Park Boulevard
Baldwin Park, CA 91706
800-258-6261
213-960-1884/818-960-1884

Cruise America
5959 Blue Lagoon Drive, Suite 250
Miami, FL 33126
800-327-7778 (from the U.S.)
800-327-7799 (from Canada)

Go Vacations Ltd.
R.R. #3, Highway 50
Bolton, Ontario
Canada LOP 1AO
416-857-6281

U-Haul International
RV Rental Division
2727 N. Central Avenue
Phoenix, AZ 85036
800-821-2712

Appendix B

RV CATEGORIES
Recreation Vehicle Industry Association
(Descriptions, Price Ranges, and Average Retail Prices—1986)

A recreation vehicle is a towable or motorized vehicle that provides transportation and temporary living quarters for travel, recreation, and camping.

TOWABLE VEHICLES

Travel Trailer
    A trailer designed to be towed by a motorized vehicle (auto, van, or pickup truck) and of such size and weight as not to require a special highway movement permit. It is designed to provide temporary living quarters for recreational, camping, or travel use and does not require permanent on-site hookup. At the campground, the tow vehicle can be detached and used for local travel. Most are equipped with their own power sources, and all have electric and water hookups. A travel trailer can be one of the following types.

    $5,000–$36,000/average $12,920

Conventional Travel Trailer   Ranges typically from 12 feet to 35 feet in length and is towed by means of a bumper or frame hitch attached to the towing vehicle.

   **$14,000–$26,000/average $16,566**

Park Trailer   Designed for seasonal or temporary living. When set up, may be connected to utilities necessary for operation of installed fixtures and appliances. Built on a single permanent chassis mounted on wheels. Designed for setup by persons without special skills using only hand tools, which may include lifting, pulling, or supporting devices.

   **$9,000–$36,000/average $16,817**

Fifth-Wheel Travel Trailer   This unit can be equipped the same as the conventional travel trailer but is constructed with a raised forward section that allows a bilevel floor plan. This style is designed to be towed by a pickup truck equipped with a device known as a fifth-wheel hitch, mounted on the bed of the truck.

    $1,500–$8,000/average $4,017

Folding Camping Trailer   A lightweight camping unit mounted on wheels and constructed with collapsible sidewalls that fold for towing by most family cars.

    $2,000–$10,000/average $7,315

Truck Camper   A recreational camping unit designed to be loaded onto, or affixed to, the bed or chassis of a truck and then removed at the campsite, freeing the truck for local use.

MOTORIZED VEHICLES

Motor Home
     A recreational camping and travel vehicle built on or as an integral part of a self-propelled motor-vehicle chassis. Kitchen, sleeping, and bathroom facilities are directly accessible from the driver's seat. Motor homes are equipped with power sources and have the ability to store

and carry water and sewage as well as hookups. A motor home can be one of the following types.

$31,000–$300,000/average $48,613

Conventional Motor Home (Type A)   The living unit has been entirely constructed on a bare, specially designed motor-vehicle chassis.

$23,000–$27,000/average $25,757

Van Camper (Type B)   A panel-type truck to which the RV manufacturer adds any of the following conveniences: sleeping, kitchen, and toilet facilities; 110-volt hookup; fresh-water storage; city-water hookup; and a top extension to provide more headroom.

$23,000–$53,000/average $32,782

Mini Motor Home (Type C)   This unit is built on an automotive-manufactured van frame with an attached cab section of a gross vehicle weight rating of 6,500 pounds or more, with an overall height of more than 8 feet. The RV manufacturer completes the body section containing the living area and attaches it to the cab section.

$20,000–$47,000/average $30,643

Low Profile Motor Home (Type C)   This unit is built on an automotive-manufactured van frame with an attached cab section having a gross vehicle weight rating of 6,500 pounds or more, with an overall height of less than 8 feet. The RV manufacturer completes the body section containing the living area and attaches it to the cab section.

$15,000–$27,000/average $21,396

Compact Motor Home (Type C)   This unit is built on an automotive-manufactured cab and chassis having a gross vehicle weight rating of less than 6,500 pounds. It may provide any or all of the conveniences of the larger units.

Multi-Use Vehicle
    A motor vehicle designed for the transportation of people and/or property and altered by the RV manufacturer for esthetic or decorative purposes. These changes may include windows, carpeting, paneling, seats, sofas, and accessories.

    $14,500–$30,000/average $20,006

Van Conversion   A completed van chassis modified in appearance for transportation and recreational purposes.

Source: Recreation Vehicle Industry Association

Appendix C   Major Tourist Sites

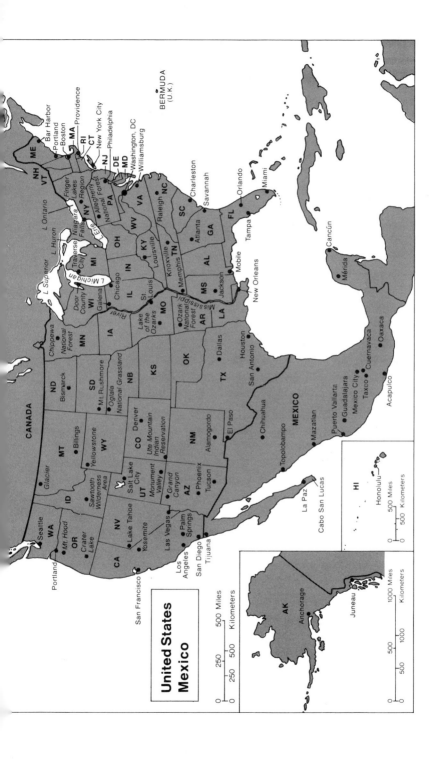

United States
Mexico

Appendix D

Federal Government Campground Offices

National Parks

U.S. Government Printing Office
Superintendent of Documents
Washington, DC 20402
Send $1.50 for "Camping in the National Park System."

National Forests

National Forest Service
U.S. Department of Agriculture
Office of Information
PO Box 2417
Washington, DC 20013

National Refuges

U.S. Fish and Wildlife Service
Public Affairs Office
Washington, DC 20240

Bureau of Land Management Sites

Bureau of Land Management
Public Affairs Office
1800 C Street, NW
Washington, DC 20240

U.S. Army Corps Projects

U.S. Army Corps of Engineers
20 Massachusetts Avenue, NW
Washington, DC 20314
Attn: Public Affairs Office

Campground Chains

Kampgrounds of America (KOA)
PO Box 30599
Billings, MT 59114
406-248-7444

Leisure Systems, Inc.
Safari/Jellystone Parks
30 N. 18th Avenue, #9
Sturgeon Bay, WI 54235
414-743-6586
For reservations, phone 800-558-2954.
For information, phone 800-358-9165.

Camp Resort Organizations

ACI Parks
12301 NE 10th Place
PO Box 1888
Bellevue, WA 98009
206-455-3155

Camp Coast to Coast
1000 16th Street, NW
Suite 840
Washington, DC 20036
202-293-8000

Leisure Systems, Inc.
30 N. 18th Avenue, #9
Sturgeon Bay, WI 54235
See phone numbers above.

Outdoor Resorts of America
2400 Crestmoor Road
Nashville, TN 37215
615-244-5237

Thousand Trails
4800 S. 188th Way
Seattle, WA 98188
206-246-5406

U.S. Vacation Resorts, Inc.
1888 Century Park, East
Los Angeles, CA 90067
213-277-9313

Campground Directories

KOA Handbook & Directory for Campers
Kampgrounds of America, Inc.
PO Box 30599
Billings, MT 59114
Free at KOA campgrounds

Rand McNally RV Park and Campground Directory
Rand McNally & Company
Box 7600
Chicago, IL 60680

Safari Campground Directory
United Safari International, Inc
30 N. 18th Avenue
Sturgeon Bay, WI 54235
Free

Trailer Life RV Campground & Services Directory
TL Enterprises
29901 Agoura Road
Agoura, CA 91301

Wheelers Recreational Vehicle Resort & Campground Guide
Print Media Services
1521 Jarvis Avenue
Elk Grove Village, IL 60007

Woodall's Campground Directories
Woodall Publishing Company
11 N. Skokie Highway
Lake Bluff, IL 60044

Appendix E

Brand-Name RV Clubs

Only owners of particular brands of RVs may belong to these clubs.

Avion Travelcade Club
1300 E. Empire Avenue
Benton Harbor, MI 49022

Barth Ranger Club
State Road 15
Milford, IN 46542
219-658-9401

Beaver Ambassador Club
10167 S.E. 45th Street
Milwaukie, OR 97722
503-659-1159

Champion Fleet Owners
  Association
5573 E. North Street
Dryden, MI 48428
313-796-2211

Cortez National
  Motorhome Club
11022 E. Daines Drive
Temple City, CA 91780

El Dorado Caravan
PO Box 266
Minneapolis, KS 67467

Elkhart Travelers National Club
2211 West Wilden Avenue
Goshen, IN 46526

Fan Trailer Club
Route #7, Box 348
New Castle, PA 16102
412-667-8264

Fireball Caravaner
12087 Lopez Canyon Road
San Fernando, CA 91342
213-896-5253

Foretravel Motorcade Club
1221 NW Stallings Drive
Nacogdoches, TX 75961

Globestar Trailer Club
1950 S. 13th Street
Niles, MI 49120

Holiday Rambler RV Club
400 Indiana Avenue
PO Box 587
Wakarusa, IN 46573
219-862-7330

International Coachmen
Caravan Club
PO Box 30, Hwy. 13 N.
Middlebury, IN 46540
219-825-8245

International Skamper
Camper Club
PO Box 338
Bristol, IN 46507
219-848-7411

Jayco Jafari
PO Box 1012
Mishawaka, IN 46544
219-258-0591

Lazy Daze Caravan Club
4303 E. Mission Boulevard
Pomona, CA 91766
714-627-1219

Midas RV Travel Club
PO Box 991
Mishawaka, IN 46544
219-258-0571

Serro Scotty Club
Arona Road
Irwin, PA 15642
412-863-3407

Silver Streak Trailer Club
226 Grand Avenue, #207
Long Beach, CA 90803

Starcraft Camper Club
PO Box 913
Mishawaka, IN 46544
219-258-0612

Wally Byam Caravan Club
International (Airstream)
803 E. Pike Street
Jackson Center, OH 45334
513-596-5211

Wings of Shasta Travel Club
PO Box 607
Goshen, IN 46526
219-534-1521

Winnebago International
Travelers
PO Box 268
Forest City, IA 50436
515-582-6874

Yellowstone National
Travelers
PO Box 951
Mishawaka, IN 46544
219-258-0591

National RV Clubs

Canadian Family Camping
 Federation
PO Box 397
Rexdale, Ontario
Canada M9W 3B3

Escapee Club
Route 5, Box 310
Livingston, TX 77351

Family Motor Coach
 Association
PO Box 44144
Cincinnati, OH 45244
800-543-3622

Good Sam RV Owners
 Club
29901 Agoura Road
Agoura, CA 91301
818-991-4980

Happy Wheelers
 International
PO Box 503
Mishawaka, IN 46544

International Travel and
 Trailer Club
15320 Crenshaw Boulevard
Gardena, CA 90249
213-329-9903

Loners on Wheels
808 Lester Street
Poplar Bluff, MO 63901

The Motorhome Travelers
 Association, Inc.
PO Box 7505
Pensacola, FL 32514
904-474-1830

National Campers & Hikers
 Association
7172 Transit Road
Buffalo, NY 14221
716-634-5433

North American Family
 Campers Association, Inc.
3 Long Hill Road
Concord, VT 05824
802-695-2563

Woodall's Travel America
 Club
11 N. Skokie Highway
Lake Bluff, IL 60044
800-826-1937

Appendix F

Canadian Provincial and Territorial Tourist Offices

Alberta

Travel Alberta
Box 2500
Edmonton, Alberta
Canada T5J 2Z4
403-427-1905

British Columbia

Tourism British Columbia
117 Wharf Street
Victoria, BC
Canada VSW 2Z2
604-387-6417

Manitoba

Travel Manitoba
Department 5020
Legislative Building
Winnipeg, Manitoba
Canada R3C OV8
800-665-0040

New Brunswick

Tourism New Brunswick
PO Box 12345
Fredericton, NB
Canada E3B 5C3
800-561-0123

Newfoundland

Tourism Branch
Department of
    Development
Box 2016
St. John's, Newfoundland
Canada A1C 5R8
709-737-2830

Northwest Territories

Travel Arctic
Yellowknife
Northwest Territories
Canada X1A 2L9
403-873-7200

Nova Scotia

Department of Tourism
PO Box 130
Halifax, Nova Scotia
Canada B3J 2M7
902-424-5000
800-341-6096 from the
    United States except Hawaii,
    Alaska, Maine
800-492-0643 from Maine only

Ontario

Ontario Travel
77 Bloor Street W
Toronto, Ontario
Canada M7A 2R9
800-268-3735 from all of
North America

Prince Edward Island

Visitor Services Division
Department of Finance and
Tourism
PO Box 940
Charlottetown, Prince
Edward Island
Canada C1A 7M5
902-892-2457
800-561-0123 from March to
August

Quebec

Tourisme Quebec
CP 20000
Quebec, Quebec
Canada G1K 7X2
514-873-2015
800-443-7000 from eastern
United States

Saskatchewan

Tourism Saskatchewan
2103 11th Avenue
Regina, Saskatchewan
Canada S4P 3V7
306-565-2300

Yukon

Tourism Yukon
PO Box 2703
Whitehorse, Yukon
Canada 61A 2C6
403-667-5430

National Parks

Parks Canada
Ottawa, Ontario
Canada K1A 1G2

For information on travel
throughout Canada, write
to the following:

Tourism, Canada
4th Floor E
235 Queen Street
Ottawa, Ontario
Canada K1A OH6

Appendix G

For general travel information on Mexico, write to the following:

Mexico Tourism
PO Box 8013
Smithtown, NY 11787

For answers to specific questions about travel in Mexico, contact the following:

Western Region, U.S. and Canada

Mexican Government
Tourist Office
10100 Santa Monica
Boulevard, Suite 224
Los Angeles, CA 90067
213-203-8151

Mexican Government
Tourist Office
2707 North Loop West
Suite 450
Houston, TX 77008
713-880-5153

Eastern Region, U.S. and Canada

Mexican Government
Tourist Office
405 Park Avenue
Suite 1002
New York, NY 10022
212-755-7261

Mexican Government
Tourist Office
One Place Ville Marie
Suite 2409
Montreal, Quebec H3B 3M9
514-871-1052

Mexican Government
Tourist Office
Two Illinois Center
233 N. Michigan Avenue
Suite 1413
Chicago, IL
312-565-2785

Mexican Government
Tourist Office
181 University Avenue
Suite 1112
Toronto, Ontario M5H 3M7
416-364-2455

Index

About the Author

Richard Dunlop and his photographer wife, Joan, have been intrepid RVers for many years, traveling in every kind of vehicle from a covered wagon to a four-wheel-drive camper on every continent but Antarctica. Dunlop is the author of twelve books, including travel guides and nonfiction historical works, and at least three thousand magazine articles. In addition to writing, he has been an editorial consultant to Rand McNally on numerous publications including their *Road Atlas* and *Campground and Trailer Park Guide.*

A past president of the Society of American Travel Writers and the Society of Midland Authors, Dunlop also has chaired the midwestern chapter of the American Society of Journalists and Authors. He received the Grand Award and Best Domestic Travel Article Award in the Mark Twain Travel Writing Contest for two years in succession.

The Dunlops, when they are at home, live in Arlington Heights, Illinois.

AARP Books

ALONE—NOT LONELY: Independent Living for Women Over Fifty
by Jane Seskin
$6.95 / AARP member price $4.95   Order #810

CAREGIVING: Helping An Aging Loved One
by Jo Horne
$13.95 / AARP member price $9.95   Order #819

CATARACTS: The Complete Guide—from Diagnosis to Recovery—for Patients and Families
by Julius Shulman, M.D.
$7.95 / AARP member price $5.80   Order #815

THE ESSENTIAL GUIDE TO WILLS, ESTATES, TRUSTS, AND DEATH TAXES
by Alex J. Soled
$12.95 / AARP member price $9.45   Order #805

FITNESS FOR LIFE: Exercises for People Over 50
by Theodore Berland
$12.95 / AARP member price $9.45   Order #818

THE GADGET BOOK: Ingenious Devices for Easier Living
Edited by Dennis R. La Buda
$10.95 / AARP member price $7.95   Order #820

THE INSIDE TRACT: Understanding and Preventing Digestive Disorders
by Myron D. Goldberg, M.D., and Julie Rubin
$9.95 / AARP member price $6.95   Order #823

IT'S YOUR CHOICE: The Practical Guide to Planning a Funeral
by Thomas C. Nelson
$4.95 / AARP member price $3.00   Order #804

KEEPING OUT OF CRIME'S WAY: The Practical Guide for People Over 50
by J. E. Persico with George Sunderland
$6.95 / AARP member price $4.95   Order #812

LIFE AFTER WORK: Planning It, Living It, Loving It
by Allan Fromme
$6.95 / AARP member price $4.95   Order #809

LOOKING AHEAD: How to Plan Your Successful Retirement
$9.95 / AARP member price $6.95   Order #817

MEDICAL AND HEALTH GUIDE FOR PEOPLE OVER FIFTY
by Dartmouth Institute for Better Health
$14.95 / AARP member price $10.85   Order #813

THE MYTH OF SENILITY: The Truth About the Brain and Aging
by Robin Marantz Henig
$14.95 / AARP member price $10.85   Order #814

NATIONAL CONTINUING CARE DIRECTORY: Retirement
Communities with Prepaid Medical Plans
Edited by Ann Trueblood Raper
$13.95 / AARP member price $9.95   Order #807

ON THE ROAD IN AN RV
by Richard Dunlop
$8.95 / AARP member price $6.50   Order #833

THE OVER EASY FOOT CARE BOOK
by Timothy P. Shea, D.P.M., and Joan K. Smith
$6.95 / AARP member price $4.95   Order #806

PLANNING YOUR RETIREMENT HOUSING
by Michael Sumichrast, Ronald G. Shafer, and Marika Sumichrast
$8.95 / AARP member price $6.50   Order #801

POLICY WISE: The Practical Guide to Insurance Decisions for
Older Consumers
by Nancy H. Chasen
$5.95 / AARP member price $4.35   Order #803

RETIREMENT EDENS OUTSIDE THE SUNBELT
by Peter A. Dickinson
$10.95 / AARP member price $7.95   Order #829

THE SLEEP BOOK: Understanding and Preventing Sleep Problems
in People Over 50
by Ernest Hartmann, M.D.
$10.95 / AARP member price $7.95   Order #832

SUNBELT RETIREMENT
by Peter A. Dickinson
$11.95 / AARP member price $8.50   Order #822

SURVIVAL HANDBOOK FOR WIDOWS (and for relatives and
friends who want to understand)
by Ruth J. Loewinsohn
$5.95 / AARP member price $4.35   Order #808

THINK OF YOUR FUTURE: Preretirement Planning Workbook
$24.95 / AARP member price $18.25   Order #826

TRAVEL EASY: The Practical Guide for People Over Fifty
by Rosalind Massow
$8.95 / AARP member price $6.50   Order #811

239 WAYS TO PUT YOUR MONEY TO WORK
by Ferd Nauheim
$8.95 / AARP member price $6.50   Order #821

WALKING FOR THE HEALTH OF IT: The Easy and Effective
Exercise for People Over 50
by Jeannie Ralston
$6.95 / AARP member price $4.95   Order #824

WHAT TO DO WITH WHAT YOU'VE GOT: The Practical Guide
to Money Management in Retirement
by Peter Weaver and Annette Buchanan
$7.95 / AARP member price $5.80   Order #800

A WOMAN'S GUIDE TO GOOD HEALTH AFTER 50
by Marie Feltin, M.D.
$12.95 / AARP member price $9.45   Order #825

YOUR VITAL PAPERS LOGBOOK
$4.95 / AARP member price $2.95   Order #181

For complete information write AARP Books, 1900 East Lake
Avenue, Glenview, IL 60025 or contact your local bookstore.

Prices subject to change.

Scott, Foresman and the American Association of Retired Persons have joined together to bring you AARP Books. *It's information you can count on.*

833. **On the Road in an RV:** Traveling in a Recreation Vehicle. *$8.95/AARP member price $6.50.*

800. **What to Do with What You've Got:** The Practical Guide to Money Management in Retirement. *$7.95/AARP member price $5.80.*

805. **The Essential Guide to Wills, Estates, Trusts and Death Taxes.** *$12.95/AARP member price $9.45.*

807. **National Continuing Care Directory:** Retirement Communities with Prepaid Medical Plans. *$13.95/AARP member price $9.95.*

808. **Survival Handbook for Widows** (and for relatives and friends who want to understand). *$5.95/AARP member price $4.35.*

810. **Alone · Not Lonely:** Independent Living for Women Over Fifty. *$6.95/AARP member price $4.95.*

811. **Travel Easy:** The Practical Guide for People Over 50. *$8.95/AARP member price $6.50.*

813. **Medical and Health Guide for People Over Fifty.** *$14.95/AARP member price $10.85.*

817. **Looking Ahead:** How to Plan Your Successful Retirement. *$9.95/AARP member price $6.95.*

181. **Your Vital Papers Logbook.** *$4.95/AARP member price $2.95.*

Join AARP today and enjoy valuable benefits

65% of dues is designated for Association publications. Dues outside continental U.S.: $7 one year, $18 three years. Please allow 3 to 6 weeks for receipt of membership kit.

Join the American Association of Retired Persons, the national organization which helps people like you, age 50 and over, realize their full potential in so many ways! The rewards you'll reap with AARP will be many times greater than your low membership dues. And your membership also includes your spouse!

☐ *START MY MEMBERSHIP IN AARP*

☐ one year / $5
☐ three years / $12.50 (saves $2.50)
☐ ten years / $35 (saves $15)

☐ Check or money order enclosed, payable to AARP. DO NOT SEND CASH
☐ Please bill me

Name (please print)   L3AA

Address   Apt.

City   L3NA

State   Zip

Date of Birth _____ mo / _____ day / _____ year

☐ *Start my membership in NRTA (a division for those in or retired from education)*

818. **Fitness for Life:** Exercises for People Over 50. *$12.95 / AARP member price $9.45.*

819. **Caregiving:** Helping an Aging Loved One. *$13.95 / member price $9.45.*

820. **The Gadget Book:** Ingenious Devices for Easier Living. *$10.95 / AARP member price $7.95.*

821. **239 Ways to Put Your Money to Work.** *$8.95 / AARP member price $6.50.*

822. **Sunbelt Retirement:** The Complete State-by-State Guide. *$11.95 / AARP member price $8.50.*

824. **Walking for the Health of It.** The Easy and Effective Exercise for People Over 50. *$6.95 / AARP member price $4.95.*

826. **Think of Your Future.** Preretirement Planning Workbook. *$24.95 / AARP member price $18.25.*

829. **Retirement Edens Outside the Sunbelt.** *$10.95 / member price $7.95.*

HOW TO ORDER

To order state book name and number, quantity and price (AARP members: be sure to include your membership no. for discount) and add $1.75 *per entire order* for shipping and handling. *All orders must be prepaid.* For your convenience we accept checks, money orders, VISA and MasterCard (credit card orders must include card no., exp. date and cardholder signature). *Please allow 4 weeks for delivery.*

Send your order today to:
AARP Books / Scott, Foresman and Co., 1865 Miner Street
Des Plaines, IL 60016

AARP Books are co-published by AARP and Scott, Foresman and Co., sold by Scott, Foresman and Co. and distributed to bookstores by Farrar, Straus and Giroux.

AARP
BOOKS

Join AARP today and enjoy valuable benefits

NO POSTAGE
NECESSARY
IF MAILED
IN THE
UNITED STATES

BUSINESS REPLY MAIL

FIRST CLASS   PERMIT NO. 3132   LONG BEACH, CA

POSTAGE WILL BE PAID BY ADDRESSEE

American Association of Retired Persons
Membership Processing Center
P.O. Box 199
Long Beach, CA 90801-9989